WILD ACRES

HENRY HAZLITT KOPMAN

WILD ACRES

A BOOK OF THE GULF COAST COUNTRY

WITH A FOREWORD BY

JOHN KIERAN

NEW YORK

E. P. DUTTON & COMPANY, INC.

1946

American Book–Stratford Press, Inc., New York

To my Wife,
who has shared my interests,
and
in memory of my Mother,
who first inspired and encouraged them.

FOREWORD

NATURE, *said Wordsworth, never did betray the heart that loved her, and many good books are ample testimony thereof. Most of the books that treat of Nature or some division of that wide field were undertaken by the authors largely as labors of love. The distinctive flavor of such books is the evident enjoyment that the authors took in the scenes recalled or the experiences recounted. There grows upon the reader the conviction that the honest intention of a writer on Nature is to share his treasures with other men and women. And children, too. It is, from the beginning, a generous gesture. This is another such book, written with quiet enthusiasm and leisurely charm out of long experience in a picturesque region, the lower reaches of the Mississippi where that great river spreads itself through the Delta into the Gulf of Mexico. The birdlife of that area is the main topic of the book.*

There is, to be sure, a notable array of bird books on public library shelves and in thousands of homes, but to those who might question the necessity or even the propriety of adding another, it may be answered that there is always room for one more good book on any attractive subject and, furthermore, in poetic vein—because all poets must be lovers of Nature—

Who can fear
Too many stars, though each in heaven shall roll;
Too many flowers, though each shall crown the year?

Foreword

Therefore, a benison on this book, through the chapters of which the reader will go on alluring excursions, led by a kindly guide who describes with scientific accuracy and literary charm the scenery and wildlife of the Wild Acres *he has known so well and loved so long.*

JOHN KIERAN

CONTENTS

[9]

Contents

REALM OF DIVERSITY:

A Word of Introduction

It is the purpose of these sketches to convey a certain spell of the open that clings to the neighborhood of the lower Mississippi and adjoining Gulf Coast country and to uncover the strange pageantry of bird life in these illusive surroundings. If the author has captured some of the scenes that lie beyond everyday horizons and at least a breath of places still belonging to the wilds, he will have satisfied some part of his expectation.

Viewing the coast realm in a spirit of passing relaxation or with absorbing attachment, a surveyor of its expanses will not find all its magic persuasion exposed at one time. Both the satisfaction of the definable and the promise of widening pictures mingle perpetually in its prospects. The outlook changes unaccountably from dimly marked shores of lakes or bays to woodland edges scrawled more visibly across the marshlands, and shifts sometimes between pineries that seem planted firmly and bayou or small river in the velvety, flexible foil of cypresses. Such in broad outline is an irresistible country. Once it is comprehended in all its versatile expression, it cannot be forgotten.

WILD ACRES

CHAPTER I

Distinction of the Lowlands

IT TAKES bright, hot days to make the most out of some
Gulf Coast scenes. The pine-clad shores of Mississippi
have their always strong outlines and colors. Marshy
and swampy lowlands of Louisiana are another matter;
unless they have the touch of light and contrast, they
revert to a dull, flat blend of unemphatic elements. The
acme of lowland individuality is the riotous growth of
aquatic plants, rising from a glossy surface of marsh or
water's edge. These and the water-loving trees of the
swamplands are the intrinsic materials of Louisiana
coastal pictures. Summer heat and light are the agents
that convert them into a glowing but perishable wealth
of scenic values.

An explorer of the fascinating, marshy wastes soon
learns their charm. In succeeding bends of a bayou,
variation of the surface is strangely interesting. The
engrossing novelty of this untouched environment rises
to a new height with the appearance of cautiously
moving or suddenly exposed birds of the marsh. Now

a least bittern, like a golden-tawny phantom, lifts itself unheralded above the surrounding growths of the marsh, settles into a brief, wavering flight at the same level, and drops with equal abruptness into the seclusion from which it ventured when an intruder was too close. Rails peer from among the matted stems of grasses and sedges growing in the semi-liquid surface of the marsh or retreat decisively, with calculated speed and a kind of unhurried elusiveness, from an open border of ooze. An almost incredibly gaudy marsh bird, the purple gallinule, bursts in an awkwardly acrobatic flight from the web of vegetation or half runs and half walks across the mud and water to escape detection.

Herons, though keeping greater distances, are in sight oftener than the low-dwelling marsh birds. Unless seen at their rookeries, they appear as single birds or small companies feeding in wide, shallow lagoons or strung out in flight over the marsh. The Louisiana heron is the most strikingly marked of its tribe frequenting these places. Its tricolor of slaty blue, white, and purplish maroon will distinguish it at considerable distances. The massing of these birds in nesting colonies among the marsh elders or low willows that grow in some parts of the marsh is a surprising spectacle. When their domain is invaded, they rise in wave after wave from the bushes that hold their nests. Any of the young old enough to leave the nests climb or flap from one perch to another, and soon more of these than of the parents are close at hand. The latter labor in swinging flight above or near the site of the colony; they seem reluctant to move away yet are caught in a dilemma of helplessness, voiced by more or less croaking and hoarse whistling. The scene becomes a distinctive episode of the marsh and one that leaves an observer long conscious of its strange participants.

Lines of swampy woodland are etched deeply in the sunshine of summer months. Seen from without, the impenetrable cushion of cypress and other foliage absorbs the light to remain a rich, dark foil against the sky or the lighter verdure of marshes, fields, and thickets. From a distance it is a smoky blue or purple band across the face of the country. The recesses of these swamps have also their distinctive character. A subdued but well-entrenched life of birds, snakes, amphibians, and insects proceeds unfailingly in the leafy, breathless shades.

In many parts of lowland Louisiana, the view swings constantly to open prospects, revolving about the smoothness of cypress-bordered lakes and the faint distances of open marshlands. A fluid coloration often broadens the view, so that some of the sharper details, as a cluster of small live oaks on bayou bank or low knoll at the edge of a boggy savanna, are inseparable parts of the general spaciousness. It is only where wide, prairie-like marshes are surrounded by heavily wooded swampland that the effect of both breadth and substance comes into existence; a sweeping and definite picturesqueness is the result. The outlines and perspectives of such a panorama are singularly imposing. It is a composition of distinct and commanding scenic qualities, not merely a conglomeration of unchecked growths in a watery, fertile region that expands without barrier over distances beyond the reach of the human eye. The great cove west of Bayou des Allemands, known generally as the "Grand Prairie," is the finest example of such scenery in southern Louisiana of which the writer knows. This open, rounded expanse of rich marshland, deeply cushioned in low, grassy growths and girdled with dense, swampy woodlands, would contain nearly any large city and its outskirts. It spreads like a great, uniform meadow to the far-off, rolling borders of cypresses. In colors and coherence it rivals a broad view in the mountains or the sight of a bold, inviting coast.

To have real familiarity with the coastal region of Louisiana is the opportunity only of professional naturalists or others whose occupations keep them continually or for long periods in these surroundings. When, in other circumstances, they recall scenes of this kind, their mental pictures must be of such retreats as the farthest reaches of rarely visited bayous in the safe interior of a great, marshy island. No suggestion of anything but its bird inhabitants and their placid-seeming haunts has penetrated here. It is an absorbing place on a sunny winter day. Not a stem of the now dry marsh grasses and rushes seems disturbed, nothing but the feather of a duck or a rail floats on the water. Red-breasted snipe, or dowitchers, huddling in a small flock on the oozy bank, are characteristic of such surroundings. So are the green-winged teal, ring-necked ducks, or blackjacks, or other lovers of quiet water that swim from behind a point with confident caution but no sign of the frenzied terror they would exhibit out in the open hunting grounds. Natural enemies, doubtless, are everywhere, but to the human eye, at least, nothing could seem more ordered and freer from the imminence of disaster or destruction.

A fastness in the remoter swamps of the Atchafalaya River is another scene that might come from memories of the Louisiana wilderness. The cypresses there rise like ancient walls, dark and rich in color and enclosing softly burnished panels of water. Wood ducks, singly, in pairs, or in little strings, fly with graceful, hardly changing speed and directness among the gaps in the treetops, in perfect command of a haunt in which few disturbances come to them. Such recesses are also the home of water-turkeys, large white egrets, wood ibises, and little blue and night herons. There is silence at most times and somber behavior among most of the birds.

Nesting colonies of sea birds are something apart

from other wild-life scenes in the coast region. Nothing but the expanse of waters, a bare foothold of sand, silt, shells, drift, and sometimes the repetitious growth of a few kinds of herbs or low shrubs form the setting. It is a simple, elemental picture in which the birds, of course, are the most conspicuous feature. Their incessant cries, their dazzling plumage, largely white in gulls and most terns, and their tireless, bewildering flight overhead as they wheel, sweep, and float in ever-shifting clouds, are the essence of turmoil.

Owing to the variations in lowland surfaces and irregularity of cultivation, the flavor of the wilds is predominant in many accessible prospects. The freedom of marsh, beach, and prairie and the silence of swamps hover over many miles of country not beyond ordinary reach. It is not absolutely primitive, but it shows all the age-old and enduring evidences of nature.

CHAPTER II

Seaside Birds and Islands

To REACH open water from the first land continuously above tide level in Louisiana requires a prolonged, almost imperceptibly changing, and often fascinating procedure. Despite superficial appearances of vagueness, however, there is a point somewhere in the stages of this transition at which seaside influences become a reality. The last fresh or brackish marshes lie behind; the tide moves among sharply outlined rushes and grasses of a salt marsh. Drift from the Gulf floats against a low, narrow bank of sand or shells; salt-water fish break above the surface of the shallow bay opening broadly into the Gulf. From such borderlines of change to the outer reaches of reefs and islands offshore, the realm belongs undisputedly to maritime birds and other life. Even the ubiquitous red-winged blackbirds and boat-tailed grackles of the marsh, especially the former, are present only incidentally. The seaside sparrow is the only passerine species with a consistent habitat in the greater part of this zone.

The life of seaside sparrows in the salt-water growths invaded regularly by the tide is one of the striking peculiarities of the outer coastal reaches. On summer mornings and evenings, these birds perch on the marsh grass stems a foot or less above the water and, singing in unison, deliver a brief, monotonous little lay. It is hardly more than a repetition of monosyllables and has the mechanical strain of the notes of the black-throated bunting: "Chig-chig-chig—chig—chig." The birds seem to love the borders of the grassy spaces for these performances, and there, in the extended formation of an orchestra, they pump out their strange notes with persistent vigor. This performance has probably fewer listeners than that of almost any other species of North American bird, for while the typical Louisiana race of the seaside sparrow is a numerous one, its habitat is a region where few persons, especially those with an interest in birds, are likely to go. Besides its more usual song, this bird has a flight song decidedly more musical. It resembles somewhat that of the Maryland yellow-throat. The bird utters these notes while poising a few feet over the water and grass in the vicinity of the nest.

The seaside sparrow nests principally in bushes of honey-mangrove, or Avicennia, known locally as "mangle," sometimes as "mangrove," of which the former term is a corruption. It is not truly a mangrove nor related to any of the several types of plants called

by that name but belongs in the botanical family of the verbena. It grows over tide flats and mucky islands and has a method of seed production so unusual that it would make an interesting topic in itself. The seaside sparrow makes a fairly substantial nest in a crotch of the Avicennia and, within sound of the lapping of waves and tide movements, hatches and cares for its young. It nests also in the marsh grasses.

A bird as frail as the seaside sparrow seems an anomaly among the hardy gulls, terns, and pelicans and the swift-winged, roving plovers, turnstones, willets, and various other shore birds so well adapted to a life of combat against winds, tides, and waves and the inhospitality of unsheltered beaches and open marshes and waters. It adds to the strangeness rather than to the wildness of the coast, but it gets its life from this environment and manages to conform to it.

At the beginning of June, as fresh, gustful breezes shear high or low and keep light clouds drifting across the sky, the strange expanses of water and fragments of land are steeped in enchantment. There is a pleasant uncertainty about what the weather has in store. Will an almost fall-like rarefaction of the clean, reviving air of the sea have command or will there be a drift to the full play of summer's strong but lenient moods?

The mixture of atmospheric ingredients has a tonic effect on the birds. Coast waters, beaches, and flats are alive with sea birds and shore birds. Nesting is in full progress among the terns, gulls, skimmers, and pelicans. Migratory or loitering plovers, curlews, sandpipers, and other beach birds scatter about the tide pools and inner, marshy fringes of shallows and low islands, glide swiftly and resolutely along an exposed beach, or swing out to sea in long arcs of flight to another feeding ground somewhere along the shore. Intentness, harmony, excitement, and restlessness mingle in the voices and movements of the changing and striving throng. The calls of the shorebirds are nearly all melodious and unhurried. The whistling of the plovers and curlews is especially clear and rounded, while the notes of the willet are shrillest and most vigorously delivered.

The constant cries of the laughing gull, which have in them a marked note of distress, or consternation, echo from many and varied quarters. Roughly represented, the call is "hare-hare," but it has many repetitions and variations and is protracted often into a series of wild, cackling cries. It is a concerted and vehement outburst conveyed but not tempered by laughter and might be directed against the entire order of existence.

Terns have less intensive, less varied calls than the laughing gulls, and in general their notes are in a higher, or lighter, pitch. A small flock of the least terns, passing airily on the summer breezes, leave a trail of chittering sounds that match the puffy winds and light spray of a perfect June day on the coast. Other species,

such as the royal and Forster terns, have screaking notes, like the sounds of rigging on a boat about to get under sail.

Although the air may be filled with these birds and numbers of them may sit in rows or other trim formations on spits and sand bars, they are most amazing at their nesting places. As there are comparatively few surfaces in this area more or less safe from inundation by tides and waves and at the same time suitable in other respects for nesting, the crowding and commotion of the birds is sometimes indescribable. Floors of shell islands two to four feet above ordinary sea levels are favorite sites for black skimmers and some of the terns. The birds either make slight depressions in this shingle or lay their eggs on it as they find it. Sandy surfaces are also nesting places. There is little or no effort to make a definite nest; there may be a little drift or wisps of grass in the hollow that answers the purpose of one.

Royal terns form the most spectacular nesting colonies along the coast. Thousands gather on some of the shell reefs that protrude from the water in the open Gulf; on these white, narrow ledges each bird lays its two or three eggs about two feet from those of its nearest neighbors. Thus the colony has a roughly crisscross arrangement of hollows, or crude nests. The birds are on the eggs only at certain hours or in certain kinds of weather, depending to a greater or less extent on the

sun as an aid in incubation. A view of these birds sitting in orderly fashion is rather rare except at a distance of about fifty yards or more, as they take to the wing on the approach of a boat, rising with sharp notes and confused flight. There is a kaleidoscopic whirling of the white and pearly forms, set off by the black caps and handsome, dagger-like red bills. A more satisfactory inspection of the colony is possible when the young are old enough to swim but not to fly. They push off from the reef only at the last minute and in a close formation. There is less distinctness in their markings than in those of the old birds, but this does not detract from the effect of precision of their movements.

Startling peculiarities of the black skimmers distinguish them clearly in the general spectacle of sea birds nesting along the coast. Unless there is a deliberate search for their nesting grounds, a casual meeting with them is most likely in the early dawn or the dusk of evening, as these are their special feeding times. They come suddenly into view in a low, swinging flight over the water near the beach. There is a rhythmic sweep in their movements, almost as if they were swimming through the air with strong, measured strokes of their long, capable wings. So many things in their appearance and behavior are unusual that it is almost impossible to do justice to all of them on first sight.

Besides their strange flight and downward inclination of the forward parts, which is an active indication

of their frequent dipping to the water, skimmers have a striking pattern of dress and very remarkable bills. The upper parts in the adult are jet black and the lower parts silky white. The bill is one of the most unusual structures seen in any bird. It is so compressed in width as to be almost like a knife blade held with the edges in the same vertical plane; the upper part, moreover, is about half an inch shorter than the lower and may be moved up and down without movement of the lower mandible. The purpose of the shape and structure of the bill, apparently, is to allow the bird to submerge the lower mandible at a shallow and fixed angle to the water, in that way reducing resistance; thus, instead of the lower part being depressed to enter the water, it shears it almost horizontally, while the necessary gaping of the bill is accomplished by raising of the upper mandible. It is from this unique adaptation that the bird gets the popular names of "shearwater" and "scissors-bill."

Just how the skimmer can pick up small shrimp, fish, and other sea life on the thin edge of its lower mandible has had no satisfactory explanation, yet the constant dipping seems to prove that this is its principal manner of feeding. There is some evidence to show that it feeds while resting on tide flats or in very shallow water, and it is said that it uses its flat bill at times to open small bivalves. The shape of the bill certainly suggests an oyster knife. The bill is black except for the basal part of the lower mandible, and this is a bright vermilion, which gives the skimmer a touch of gaudiness to go with what looks like a full-dress suit, a costume that adds powerfully to the generally strange effect of a bizarre bird character. Even with all these peculiarities, the skimmer has at least one other strange and distinctive trait—its note, which is almost incredibly like the yapping of a small dog. If one were not in sight of the birds as they drive along above the water, it would be easy to suppose that a little pack of dogs had run across the trail of a rabbit or other small animal and were pursuing it closely.

In their anatomy and habits, aside from some of the peculiarities mentioned, skimmers have a good deal in common with terns. They nest in the same manner, usually on open sand or shells but, as a rule, somewhat apart from nesting colonies of other species. They are most conspicuous, however, not on their nests but as they gather to rest in clear-cut platoon formations on spits, bars, and smooth beaches. Their black upper parts make them extremely prominent even at considerable distances. They do not crowd very closely, so that if they are seen from a slight elevation, the outlines of many of the birds are distinguishable. The whole flock is more or less oblong, and its curving contours match the lines of beaches and coves that make up the surrounding perspectives.

Outer beaches of the more important islands are undisturbed resorts of wandering shorebirds characteristic of this season. It is nesting time here for a few, but many more seem to have no well-defined place in the yearly round of bird existence. Some may continue to migrate to more northern breeding grounds, yet others may stay all summer without mating. Most of the latter, no doubt, are birds hatched the preceding summer and not yet in their fullest sexual vigor. In their ranks may be some "bachelors," males that have found no mates or possibly are less imbued than usual with the instinct of propagation. By preference or otherwise they do not give up regularly their life of free movement for more fixed habits. The black-bellied plover, for instance, is not known to nest in Louisiana, yet birds in fine plumage are on many of the beaches throughout the early summer, when individuals that will breed may be presumed to have left for more northern localities. Thus, while not nesting in this latitude, this handsome, sturdy, but rather shy species is very much a part of the summer bird life. Single birds and little flocks, halting briefly or running rapidly and easily along the surf-packed gray sand, are one of the inspiring sights of a radiant early summer day. The clear notes are constantly in the air.

The Wilson plover, less striking in size and markings than the black-bellied plover, is a true native of this region. It is a consistently familiar inhabitant of the beaches and is in this latitude because it nests here.

It is known best on the true sea beaches, where it feeds almost within touch of the surf. It may nest either singly or in small colonies, depositing its eggs in a very slight depression on the sand or shells, sometimes scarcely beyond reach of the tide, or in other cases in grassy places a little farther back from the beach. In the latter instance, the eggs may be concealed partially. Regardless of the situation of the nest, the eggs blend more or less closely with the surroundings and, like the young, are hard to detect. The latter, of course, begin to run about as soon as hatched. The Wilson plover is one of the ring-necked group and, except for its duller coloration, resembles a small killdeer. It is about the color of very wet sand above, is white below, and has a black collar.

Variations of haunts for the birds of the Louisiana seacoast are numerous. Extremes are the Chandeleur group of islands, which are not only extensive but lie farthest from the coast and are maritime in every respect, and Grand Isle, west of the mouth of the Mississippi River, which differs from all the others in being higher, wider, and more fertile and, therefore, fit for settlement and planting. Besides many large live oaks, there is a great deal of vegetation on it. Grand Isle is not a place suited to the nesting of sea birds but a resting and feeding spot for the smaller migratory birds in spring after a flight across the Gulf of Mexico. Here among oaks, wax myrtles, yaupons, and transplanted or naturalized oleanders, oranges, and other shrubs and small trees surprising troops of migrants settle for a few days. Some species that seldom tarry on their way through Louisiana in spring concentrate here and are much at home during their usually brief stay. The rose-breasted grosbeak sometimes in late spring is as common on Grand Isle as far more familiar species. Some of the rarer warblers and flycatchers make their most regular appearances on this favorably situated landing place. In fall, their flight across the Gulf being ahead of them instead of behind them, they have no special incentive to collect here.

In the marsh along the western coast of Louisiana there are several "chenières," which are ridges covered with the same native growth as on Grand Isle and serve as stopping places for the same kinds of birds. The geologically peculiar "islands" on or near the border between marsh and prairie in southwestern Louisiana are merely wooded hills that rise from the level surfaces and attract birds that inhabit a somewhat similar environment farther inland. Swampy places about one of these formations—Avery Island—have become noted as a sanctuary for the snowy heron, once threatened with extinction, and for other aquatic species.

CHAPTER III

Wonders of a Day

A LATE APRIL DAY of rarefied light and color and a miraculously blended sensation of mildness and freshness in the air occasions intense displays of small, migratory birds on their way through the Gulf Coast zone. Secrets of their travels are surrendered carelessly with the incitement of atmospheric perfection of foliage in its first full richness. Birds strangely absent except at such times flash into view with a convincing, if transitory, proof of their existence. The peculiar, ethereal weather conditions are at the same time an admonition of cooler weather beyond the point at which the birds have arrived in their northward progress and are an environment exactly suited to their fastidious and sensitive vitality. They are in a state of precipitation in a region that provides temporarily the circumstances to which they react with greatest liveliness and confidence. Their presence lasts for only a day or so, and they vanish with the atmospheric change that brought them.

Warm nights, especially if there is no wind nor rain, encourage the migrants to press on as far and as fast as possible. Thus they may reach points well inland, up to a hundred miles or at least beyond the low coast belt. It is only when they meet cooler weather or other atmospheric disturbances at the time of their arrival on or near the coast that they fall short of the objectives of the first night's flight inland and frequent spots in which they would never appear under other circumstances. If these happen to be especially attractive to them at the time, as in the case of some of the oak-wooded ridges and islands of the coast, they may linger several days before making a fresh start.

If every condition is favorable, there is a great vortex of bird life with the rising barometer and the lowered temperature, manifested by unfamiliar figures or the exuberance of customary kinds. Kingbirds, barn swallows, wood thrushes, catbirds, yellow warblers, summer tanagers, and indigo buntings, in perfect plumage, are among the rank and file. They would be a spectacle of uncommon beauty even without the rarities that mingle with them. Even as familiar a species as the orchard oriole, doubly resplendent in its rich chestnut and glistening black, recharges the attention accorded it as a never-failing figure of any spring or summer day and cannot be forgotten entirely except in a moment when a strange warbler appears in a parting of the foliage. The time is one of completeness, adding luster to the general concourse of better-known species, a passing familiarity to the strangers. The phenomenon is not peculiar to the Louisiana lowlands and contiguous country. As a matter of fact it occurs less frequently than farther north and involves more species, some of them seen so rarely that in this respect, at least, it is distinctive.

A trio of astonishing species—scarlet tanager, Baltimore oriole, and rose-breasted grosbeak—are almost as chary of an appearance in spring as certain of the warblers, are spectacular among the group of transients. Their size and bright plumage and the comparative boldness of their movements, leading them to keep in sight much of the time on the rather rare days when they are present, thrust them into prominent roles. Though not very closely related, they seem to react with much the same high-strung response to the migratory urge of the season and to live on the same level of vitality as they pause in the lightly luxuriant foliage or illuminate it with a flash of shifting color. The sight of all three species in a single tree is an experience seldom coming to an observer in the lowlands. I happened to have such a chance once, sighting them in the upper and outer branches of a mulberry, to which they were attracted, more likely, by the insects than by the first ripening fruit.

Warblers constitute the greater part of one of these exceptional migratory hosts in late April. Some are the kinds that prefer the upper foliage and are typified principally by the woodland species of *Vermivora* and *Dendroica*. The less frequently seen are black-throated green, chestnut-sided, Blackburnian, black-throated blue, golden-winged, and blue-winged. The bay-breasted and blackpoll warblers come usually at the very end of the migrations, and the former, at least, does not seem to be in the same hurry as most of the others. It is comparatively easy to see these migrants, however, as it is characteristic of their behavior for them to keep to the newer, terminal foliage, where the hunt for insects may be combined with the restless, travel-imbued energy that keeps them moving from tree to tree.

On typical April days in this latitude, when southerly breezes bring a very summery touch to the fully ver-dant surroundings, it is useless, ordinarily, to look for the purely transient birds bound from the tropics to mostly far northern breeding grounds. In many years of observation near New Orleans, I found this to be true except on one surprising occasion. The day, April 21, after starting gray and quiet, was warm, clear, and breezy; there had been no particular change in the weather for possibly a week. The most remarkable part of the experience was finding all the unexpected birds within a space of a few acres. This particularly favor-able observation ground was a loose thicket of live and water oaks of medium size that had come up on what appeared to have been well-drained plantation land at the edge of the more varied swamp woodland through which a companion and I had made our way up to this time. Among the oaks were a few hackberries, honey locusts, sycamores, and several other species of trees. The undergrowth was principally briar and smilax.

Assembled in the small, distinctive patch of woodland on which we had chanced were black-and-white, worm-eating, black-throated green, and chestnut-sided warblers, ovenbird, redstart, scarlet tanager, and rose-breasted grosbeak—eight purely transient species that we had seen nowhere else in the course of the day, besides several others that were more plentiful here than elsewhere. We had come upon an "island" of unusual growth that had something of the character of upland woods and was congenial enough to the birds now in its midst to hold them for a few days in the course of their migratory passage. Exactly what they prefer in such more open, drier woods to the close, succulent forest of ash, maple, elm, ironwood, swamp dogwood, tupelo, and box elder is not altogether clear, but it seems that the freer entrance of sunlight, contributing to an abundance of more easily found and pursued insects, may have something to do with the manifest preference of many species of birds for such growths.

CHAPTER IV

A Lasting Wilderness

THE DELTA of the Mississippi River is a remarkable panorama of broad, jumbled perspectives of water and grassy, reedy growths and suggests at once its own two greatest peculiarities. One is its detachment from all habitable surfaces of importance, and the other its unusual attractiveness for ducks and geese. The effect of these circumstances is to make it one of the most picturesque hunting grounds on the continent. Remote as it is from points beyond which land travel is impossible, it is astir in fall and winter with the spirit and activity of hunters whose enthusiasm for the scenes and shooting here is not discouraged by the length of the trip.

The story of the thronging of wildfowl to the delta and the hunting there is a mixture of opulence and primitive living, of extravagant enjoyment of this rare abundance and of the growth of means for protecting it. Professional hunters and the clubs of the wealthy have had their days in the delta grounds. Designation of special shooting and refuge areas under public control have followed eras of waste and monopoly.

No number of hunters ever able to reach the many square miles of duck grounds in the delta could crowd it, and on most hunting days there are hardly enough to keep even a small proportion of the birds shifting among the better feeding spots. Most of the hunters, however, remain within a somewhat limited radius of camping headquarters, and so the choice of favorable sites is not made as easily as the great number of birds in this general locality might indicate. Some of the guides are very expert at anticipating what conditions will be at particular points and can predict rather closely the kinds of ducks to be expected in the flights. The duck potato, tuberlike rootstock of a species of arrowhead, is a very important food in the delta expanses. Discovery of ponds or lagoons where this plant remains in considerable abundance is a matter of constant study by the more efficient guides, especially as this food is a favorite of the mallard.

In the matter of actual proximity to his fellows, a hunter in the delta finds himself usually in a scene of unmistakable solitude. Except for his guide or his hunting companion, he is in his own world of watery ooze and intricate aquatic vegetation, with the positions of other hunters at vague distances and in topographically uncertain relationships. Shots far away and infrequent, scarcely audible voices are the only things not of nature that come within the circle of his vision and hearing.

Though the delta affords so substantial an attraction for ducks, there is an element of unreality in it. It is full of mirages, not of water but of land. Closing the view across a chain of shallow waters or far along an arm of some pass or outlet to the sea, a wall of willows, marsh elders, or giant reeds creates an illusion of wooded shores. A close approach would reveal them as the most precarious of footings, the slightest mooring of drifted silt and the matted debris of plants. Where currents have ceased to flow or to spread, however, there are more substantial banks and ridges, on which the deer of this region have at least one dependable resting place.

Other bird life besides ducks is interesting in winter. Wild geese congregate about the bars and flats that make up most of the seashore, being inaccessible here to hunters on account of the shallowness of the water and lack of places for blinds. Goose-shooting is possible only when foggy or other heavy weather drives the birds over the inner waters of the delta. Most of the geese coming here are blue and lesser snow geese. They gather by thousands, various sections of the great concourse rising, wheeling, settling again. At a distance, their appearance in the air is like a bank of fog or pearly smoke over the shore.

On all but very mild, still days, most bird life concentrates in winter in the more sheltered places. Besides the ducks, there are grebes, coots, and a few herons that remain at this season. Duck hawks, prime enemies of wild fowl, and low-sailing marsh hawks, which feed sometimes on dead ducks, are striking objects over the marshy wastes. White pelicans, sailing impressively at varying heights or afloat on the broader waters, are strong figures. In rough weather loons, cormorants, pelicans, geese, and gulls are about the only kinds frequenting the seashore and open waters of the bays and passes.

The delta includes within its general boundaries the peculiar formations known as "mudlumps." They lie in the bays that border the indefinite surfaces through which the passes flow. An average mudlump is less rather than more than an acre in extent and sometimes only a few square rods. It is roughly oval or circular, has a layer-like formation, with edges abrupt or irregularly sloping, and rises seldom more than five or six feet above the level of high tide. Seen from a distance, mudlumps resemble low rocks rising from the sea. Somewhat like the waters of the Mississippi, their surface is gray or dun-colored. The soil, however, is not generally alluvial but appears to be of the same character as that of the clays in the bed of the river, suggesting to some geologists that the origin of a mudlump may be traced to subterranean pressure, like that under the salt domes of the coast. Nothing grows on these spots except a few cockleburs and other rank weeds.

Brown pelicans, Caspian and royal terns, and occasionally laughing gulls are about the only creatures that make any use of the mudlumps, which are curious but not attractive places. Pelicans, at any rate, find them very satisfactory nesting sites, and when they take possession there is very little room for anything else. Besides the pelicans that nest here many others roost on these places. In all, it is not unusual for several thousand birds to collect about the several groups of mudlumps near the main passes of the river.

Nesting of pelicans is at its height about the first of June and is an occasion of remarkable turmoil. The clamor of the young, which are hatched naked but soon acquire a whitish or light cream-colored down, their struggles to secure more than a fair share of the food brought them, and the arrival of the parents from their foraging flights are unlike anything else in the bird life of this region. The differences in the ages of earlier and later broods add to the natural confusion of a pelican colony. Newly hatched birds, scarcely able to raise their heads, others nearly ready to walk, and still older birds about ready to fly and fully capable of swimming are about their nesting island at one time.

Maritime bird life becomes conspicuous with the return of warm weather. Winter gulls begin to disappear, but laughing gulls become more prominent and widespread, gathering at their few nesting places in this vicinity or passing near the shore line on their way to and from more suitable grounds. The ranks of Caspian, royal, and other terns begin to fill up as the south winds come sweeping in from the Gulf. The center of bird life swings away from the seclusion of inner waters and grassy flats to the open, tidal spaces. While rails continue to live concealed in the marshes and gaudy gallinules and small, brightly colored bitterns have come there in place of ducks, they are not in sight as often as the many water birds swimming, wading, or flying outside the margins of the delta.

The man-o'-war bird joins the ranks of marine species during the summer. This great feathered aeronaut commands the sky over the Gulf. At least a few man-o'-war birds, soaring at great heights, each maintaining its separate course, are about on most summer days, and sometimes the number increases to scores. They may rise to heights at which they are scarcely visible. Their time of feeding depends a good deal on the movements of gulls and terns, which they rob of fish, rushing at them from above and then seizing the fish often in midair when it is dropped by the bewildered victim.

The man-o'-war bird nests on tropical shores and reaches the Gulf Coast after its breeding season. Rarer than this species and equally graceful, though not so bold in its flight, the yellow-billed tropic-bird, follower of ships, makes a casual appearance off the Mississippi delta. The bald eagle and the osprey are other figures in the concourse of seacoast birds, though rather rare ones, as there are no trees for their nesting in this watery region.

There are no suitable places in the delta for the great majority of land birds. After flights across that Gulf, small migratory birds may rest and feed in the few small trees, planted or sprung from chance seeds, that have managed to survive in the shelter of buildings. Once, in April, I saw a Blackburnian warbler, one of the most characteristic woodland species, in the marshes bordering one of the passes. I cannot recall ever seeing a bird that looked more misplaced.

CHAPTER V

Vacationist of "Nineties" Recalls Some Birds

NO OTHER EXPERIENCE through which I passed as a very youthful naturalist is quite as clear in my memory as a first acquaintance with the birds of the Mississippi coast, probably because they supplied me with an uninterrupted interest. Perennially picturesque, the coast was formerly an ideal environment for complete appreciation of nature. There was no sea wall at the time that I have in mind, and other encroachments did not go beyond the main essentials of comfortable homes, a sandy beach road, and bathing and fishing wharfs. It was just a place of summer repose, with hardly a suggestion of the tension of town or city, yet it was not a wilderness.

Vacation visits to the coast began at about the time in which light Gulf breezes started a mild commotion and pleasant rustling in the tops of the pines; when the pungence of resinous odors took on its true potency and the ground beneath the pines was studded with a great variety of simple, exact, vivid flowers. There were milkwort, its roots giving off the odor of wintergreen, yellow star-grass, sea-pink, meadow-beauty, and variously colored beach peas. Bird life was aglow with the eagerness and trustfulness that go with the most critical stages of the nesting season. Fledglings and newly hatched young kept the air and the trees vocal. They were moving endlessly among the pines and intervening oaks, cedars, pecans, mulberries, figs, and scuppernong grape arbors of homesites.

The redheaded woodpecker, its intense markings at their glossiest and in boldest contrast with the summer background, was a startling object. The crimson feathers of its head gleamed with a flowery brilliance as if newly derived from the surrounding productiveness of nature. In the midst of rare beauty and exuberance, in fact, the bird was a sort of universal measurement of richness and vitality for the entire throng of irrepressible feathered characters. Scolding, chattering, calling sonorously, and pitching into short, whirring flights as pursued or pursuer in passages of robbery, love, and quarreling staged with others of its kind, next drumming contentedly or probing for some desirable grub, it nearly dominated any scene of which it was a part. It lived up to the prominence of the blue jay and the mockingbird and outmatched them in the impact of color and nervous activity at this season.

Orchard orioles were very animated but in a less roisterous way than the redhead. They thrived in the genial, relaxing air of the coast, with its pungent, healing, and vitalizing fragrances. The fluency of their lively, sweet-pitched notes, almost a cascade of clear, simple melody, seasoned the mornings, the late afternoons, and the evenings wherever there were shade or fruit trees. The eggy-yellow young, prominently marked with golden pinfeathers and gape of beak, twittered and chippered consistently, some of them clambering, fluttering, and tumbling incessantly about their nests.

A bird that drew me to a greater fondness for the pinewoods was the brown-headed nuthatch. Its preoccupation as it climbed on the pine trunks was astonishing and was traceable even in its infrequent, short-measured, nasal-sounding notes. At other times, roving in small, loose, restless companies, birds of this species traveled through the upper parts of the trees and reflected with their faintly piping calls the wistful remoteness of the orderly, never-ending spaciousness of the pine forest.

Red-cockaded woodpeckers, of a species largely southern in distribution, were most at home where the pines were thickest. Their short, sharp, frequently repeated notes, as crisp as pine chips and sounding something like the tap of a small hammer on flint, traveled in a light cross-fire of intonations in the clean, dry woods. These birds belonged as much to their environment as the streaks of half-dried resin on the pine trunks, the empty shells of cicadas, and the "sawyers," or beetle larvae, that bored in diseased or fallen trees.

It was only after long-continued observation that I identified the author of a short, simple, musical trill that came now and then from the pine tops. Sometimes I had caught a glimpse of a small bird moving slowly and uncertainly in the lofty sprays, safe at that height from too prying eyes or attempts to secure it as a specimen with a gun of limited range or accuracy. Finally a close view of a singing bird showed it to be the pine warbler. It had a definite part in the characteristic bird life of these seashore woods yet led a rather versatile existence. Towards the end of summer, its movements in the smaller pines and adjacent scrubby oaks and its frequent presence on the littered ground beneath them gave it a role very different from that of the small musician in the crowns of pines.

Brown pelicans towards the horizon and laughing gulls and royal terns patroling inshore were always familiar sights. In middle or late July the beach at high tide and sand bars at low tide began to fill up with the advance hosts of southward bound or promiscuously wandering sandpipers and some of their larger relatives. Their animated, impulsive movements and intoned, melodious cries became the most striking sights and sounds of the shore in this stirring time of their migration. No matter how familiar their presence might be, it held a touch of mystery, a promise of novelty in their behavior from hour to hour.

To a boy with thoughts of hunting some of the larger and warier of the shore birds were tantalizing figures. An air rifle was no provision to match against the strong, sizable, alert willet. This large member of the tattler family, a sturdy figure in gray, white, and black, with the body size of a dove, seemed to him a very impressive creature. The loud, assured, whistling note with which it would take off from a sand bar when a weakly impelled shot hit near it was particularly discomfiting and embarrassing to a young hunter. It left him with that feeling of incompetence and futility known only to pursuers of wild life.

There were numerous other birds of the snipe-plover group to be seen at this time, especially yellow-legs, the now rare knot, or robin snipe, dowitchers, or red-breasted snipe, and occasional curlews. All of them, of course, were far more numerous than they are today. Except for small sandpipers and plovers, which there was no occasion nor temptation to shoot unless an identification were needed, most of them were as far out of reach as the moon.

The tameness of some of the sandpipers was extraordinary. Standing on the beach, I have known little flocks of the finger-length least and semipalmated sandpipers to feed within a few feet of me before taking flight, and on one occasion a single least sandpiper passed between my feet as I stood astride of the line of its feeding. This disregard of the presence of a human being might have been due not entirely to fearlessness but to the fact that these little creatures, looking for minute forms of life in the sand, keep their eyes downward and forward and might, in some circumstances, be oblivious of a person in their path.

The period of light, offshore winds in the morning and hot, breathless afternoons, lasting through parts of July and August, brought not only flights of shorebirds but marked changes in the ranks of land birds. The yellow warbler, a small, trim, golden silhouette as it slipped in tenuous flight across openings among oaks and pines or found half-concealment of its shining, diminutive form in cedars and scuppernong arbors, typified these days of intense summer colors. This species had nested somewhat farther north but came now in strong migratory cohorts, with true autumn temperatures still many weeks in the future. Supporting its instinct for early migration were such other small, dainty birds as the redstart and black-and-white, cerulean, prairie, and even golden-winged and black-throated green warblers, each a unique pattern of delicacy and beauty.

The little redstart absorbed much of a beginner's attention in efforts to identify it. The first that I ever saw and the only other individuals that I came across for some time were in the plumage of the adult female or of immature birds, tricked out in blotches of green, gray, dusky white, and yellow or light orange instead of the sharply outlined black, salmon-flame, and white of the old male. They careered about in the lower branches of an old live oak and seemed so peculiar in their appearance and movements that a novice in ornithology felt at a loss in relating them to more familiar species. They were just some little birds of odd character, exact knowledge of which seemed no more obtainable than if they had come from another planet. As with many other experiences in learning about the birds, the mystery cleared up when the right procedure for identification was found.

The wearing on of summer not only brought the early migrants but resulted in the disappearance or relegation to the background of some characteristic birds of the early season, notably the orchard orioles. They were no longer lively, tuneful, conspicuous but much subdued, gathering in small, loose troops, in which the young predominated. Several families united, evidently, to form these little companies, and probably most of them were from farther north. They moved uncertainly and seclusively through the smaller trees but kept up an almost constant, soft-voiced chattering, punctuated with a melodious, querulous, long-drawn note that suggested either the dependence of the young or the solicitude of parent birds for the inexperienced members of the caravan assembled for their first migratory flight across the Gulf. By the middle of August a very large proportion of them were gone, but now and then a new group would drift through these surroundings.

In the finding of new birds nothing astonished me quite as much as an apparition that confronted me suddenly one late September day as I looked into a cluster of pokeberry bushes growing by a rail fence at the edge of a little wood. A bird the size of a small thrush and with the richest orange-yellow breast I had ever seen was in plain enough view to assure me that I was about to form a new feathered acquaintance. Silent, engrossed in filling itself with the pokeberry fruit, it was a token extraordinary of the quiet, protracted, almost inscrutable passage of migrating birds in autumn. It turned out to be a yellow-breasted chat, largest member of the warbler family. Its bright olive-green back, beautiful throat and breast, and white belly made it one of the most vividly marked birds I had ever seen. A sharp, white line over the eye and a black mark before it, besides a stain or two of pokeberry juice on the underparts, gave it an even more striking appearance. It was something of a stranger and transient in this dry woodland spot, its summer home being by choice in moist thickets of low willows and other bushy tangles near water. Its muteness and sedateness at this season was in greatest contrast to its odd vocalizations and other performances in nesting time.

In the earlier pageant of migration, barn swallows

were most frequently in sight, especially on August mornings. They passed eastward along the shore in a scarcely interrupted file, following each other usually by a difference of a few seconds, no great distance as measured in the speed of their flight. Except for an occasional light "trillup, trillup," they sustained their swift flight silently. The coast, leading on to Florida and tropical shores, was a great coursing ground for them. On overcast, squally, or showery days the flight was greatest and continued with little interruption until evening. Sometimes detachments would reverse their direction, possibly because they had run into heavy weather ahead and were in search of better resting and feeding places in the stretches of the coast that they had left behind. On fine mornings, there was no remission in their space-consuming travel. Only at uncertain intervals would one swerve from its sure track and hover for a moment to take in a gnat or other small insect in the air. Even at other times their flight was in great contrast to the higher, drifting movements of nighthawks and purple martins that appeared on cloudy afternoons and evenings after rain.

It was not until the first week or so in September that the true fall migration began, taking the place of more desultory movements in the dog days. Catbirds arrived in daily growing numbers in the shadier woods, feeding on the ripened seeds of sweet bay and magnolia or on pokeberries that grew at the edges of thickets of wax myrtle, pine sapplings, small oaks, and other shrubs, trees, and vines. Their reiterated and plaintive call-notes rose on all side in these retreats, a chorus to go suitably with their dusky plumage and the tinge of somberness in autumn lights and colors. Added to the influx of catbirds were kingbirds, red-eyed vireos, and wood thrushes, swelling the numbers of those species already present. Every day brought some different bird, until by the end of September or beginning of October the leafier or swampier patches of woods dispersed among the pines were the background of a constant shifting and mingling of flycatchers, vireos, and warblers, along with large or small numbers of cuckoos, tanagers, thrushes, and others less frequently expected. Altogether, they made up one of the most diversified and salient bird assemblages ever present in this tranquil region.

CHAPTER VI

Ship Island: Marine Frontier

IN AN ERA ending with the general introduction of motorboats it had been a custom among summer vacationists on the Mississippi coast to arrange "schooner parties" for a day's fishing and sightseeing at Ship Island, ten miles offshore and largest of several sandy, pine-tufted barriers sheltering Mississippi sound from the open waters of the Gulf. Such affairs were entirely masculine. With head winds from a southerly quarter, the sail to the island was a choppy one and a period of great wretchedness for any landlubber who managed to have himself included in the excursion, which was on a basis of congeniality or, at least, favorable acquaintance.

I remember a young man from the hills of Georgia who joined one of these fishing parties and became so violently seasick about halfway to the destination that there was serious consideration of turning back, not for the safety of his physical being but for his feelings and those of the unafflicted. He managed, however, to recall himself sufficiently from the depths of his misery to indicate disagreement with such a decision. As it would have taken almost as long to get back as to continue to a landing at the island, his willingness to stick it out settled the issue. With what cheer his fellow cruisers could give him, he passed through another hour or so of limp and groaning prostration and was revived only when the schooner came into the quieter waters behind the island, to be helped ashore in an erect position, hoping and praying that he would react with less serious distress on the return trip. That it turned out so might have been one of the reasons for his encouragement to continue his theological studies, which resulted later in his becoming a noted divine.

If the rough waters had been a new sensation to the inexperienced student, there were others aboard who were to find a first realization of the meaning of the sea, its constancy and inexhaustibility, the breadth and depth of its self-containment, self-renewal, and resistance against change. Sometimes its full influence reached to the shallow waters left behind, but here its sway was unending. Only the island about which it lapped and washed gave man any permanent right in the open sweep of the Gulf. The lighthouse and the square-riggers at the weathered, salt-soaked, heavily built wharf were the only things not of natural origin on which human existence could be hinged. Odors of tar, old rigging, wet sacking, fish refuse, and stale food and liquor managed to cling about the ladders and lower stagings of the wharf, but everywhere else the air was clean with the salt of the sea.

Around the great pilings under the wharf was a cavernous space above the water, shot with rays of light sifting through the crevices of the timbers. It was here that most of the fishermen of a schooner party elected to spend their time matching strategy and skillful quickness with wily, nimble spadefish and sheephead feeding in deep shadows about the pilings. It was a sport full of tense expectations and suspense, quick, decisive culminations, and, of course, mischances. The splendors of the shadowy, cool-looking waters, perfectly limpid and an ambered shade of green at the surface, darkening in the dimmer layers, lent a particular fervor to the enjoyment. A fisherman might wonder what was going on in the briny vaults beneath, muse over the numbers and behavior of strong and untethered forms rushing this way and that in their impenetrable element—jackfish, sharks, rays, jewfish, and other great creatures of the deeper waters. Only the lesser prey and satellites of these formidable inhabitants of the sea, like the bright-colored grunts and small sheephead, switched momentarily against the pilings within the zone of invading light and then, darting suddenly downward, dissolved into the nothingness of darkness below.

Those who fished in more open water off the end of

the island in the hope of battles with tarpon, large red-fish, Spanish mackerel, and other fine fighters that chances of the sea might bring their way had less as-surance of success than with the fish about the pilings. They were certain, at least, of a more strenuous attempt, involving heavy tackle and exposure in a skiff or yawl to the fiery brightness of the sun on the rock-ing, green waters of the inner Gulf. Any moment might mean the expected struggle with a hard-yielding, gal-vanic rover of the open sea, coldly, unimpressionably compacted of fin, scale, muscle, and propeller-like tail fit to test the nerves and resistance of the stoutest angler. It could result in final triumph for him or in broken rod, snapped line, strained reel, or tearing loose of hook from the iron jaw that had closed on it. Most of those who came back from such encounters, arms and faces retinted in the chromatic shades of a scalded crab, were ready for the comforts and restorations of the schooner's deck or the supply of food and drink.

To complete the wonder of a day at the island, there was the slowly heaving surf that curls on the wide, beveled slope of the outer beach. Here were such stranded curiosities as medusas, king crabs, and strange shells, disconnected objects in the never-ending story of infinitely varied marine life. Out in the green, trans-parent water, bright blue and red crabs, darkly varie-gated turtles, and companion life of subtropic seas lay or moved in perfect clarity of detail on the pale, sandy bottom. They were part of a disclosure of the sea in all its unity of existence and complexity of production, not overwhelming in this manifestation of its mystery but bright and mild, with an irresistible display of beauty.

CHAPTER VII

In and Out with the Calendar

EVEN IN FULL SPRING and summer there are days in the
Gulf Coast country that lack the character of their
seasons; as for other times, it is often puzzling to make
out the calendar from the quality of the weather. A
day of just the kind that might be expected at any
particular point in the yearly cycle is thus likely to be
memorable. It marks sometimes a seasonal turning
point, as when late summer warmth, with only the
hazy glint of shimmering air to suggest the sparkle of
autumn, makes way overnight for the first briskness
and clear delineations in every scene.

There is quickening in the life of birds after a break
in the lethargy of summer heat, broods of fresh-colored
butterflies are abroad, and minor symptoms of change
and travel reach the surface. They are only intimations
of more compelling transitions to come. Though the
heat may return and though, on the other hand, there
have been evidences of early bird migration for some
weeks past, the first distinct signals of an autumnal

cast have been displayed over water and clouds and in fields, woods, and marsh. A heavier haze hangs over the horizon at sunset, nighthawks and swifts thread the sky towards dusk in growing numbers, martins travel in an ever-increasing intensity of southward flight.

For a fortnight or so after this first measurable prospect of autumn, nothing else distinguishes most of the days from those of late summer. The equinoctial date comes nearest at Gulf Coast latitude to bringing on autumnal conditions. Flowers of ironweed and goldenrod begin to replace summer blooms, the tints of verdure show a turn to the less luxuriant shades of fully ripened leaves. Summer birds yield possession of their rallying places to conspicuously active migrants. The whole change of the seasons goes on quietly but unmistakably, and when its first impulse is over, the picture defined is one clearly different in some of its details.

The weather of October is the most constant in the round of the Gulf Coast seasons. There are no signs of either tension or of sharp change in the ample days, some brisk, others bland. The turn from summer being conclusive, a period of drifting sets in, expressed in a mild maturity and easy energy, the first touch of fall coloring in the foliage, the loitering of migratory birds, the staging of a final carnival of variegated brightness among the butterflies. There are pleasantly warm days, a few on the verge of frostiness, mild skies, woods and fields still fully clothed with vegetation, loose cohorts of white-breasted tree swallows, rising and falling or floating and scudding lightly before gentle, vagrant winds like the smooth, bright clouds above them. Sometimes a chance wedge of geese pushes on in wavering, persistent flight to a first landing in the marshes.

Though rains and light frosts or even colder weather come in November and all birds not forming part of the winter assemblage have left for a warmer clime, much of the month is often a pale likeness of October. A generally brown, yellow, or bright russet cast spreads over lowland woods, relieved by the evergreen oaks and the more brightly tinted leaves of maple and sweet gum, to which are added in the higher pinewoods country the deep wine-red leaves of the black gum. The leaves of some trees are falling rapidly or are all gone. In the sharper light of a clear, cold day, the imprint of winter seems strong enough, while on a mild day, with its mellow radiance, there is the fullness of tempered colors more varied than those of summer. This phantom beauty in the countryside cannot be compared well with that of any other season and is, in reality, a peculiar creation of the subtropical autumn.

Most or all of the leaves on deciduous trees have fallen and other vegetation sensitive to cold has died down by early December, but what is left, with any evergreen growth and the bright trunks and branches of trees, is sufficient to create in the warm, sunny weather an illusion only slightly removed from the reality of spring or summer. Plants cannot change as quickly as the temper of the air and the light, but most birds seem capable of doing so, especially those that have sought these surroundings for the harsher part of the year. Many come out of the shelter of thickets, briars, and bushy places to a wider scene of activity, and a few, particularly the ruby-crowned kinglet, white-throated sparrow, and hermit thrush, even utter fragments of their songs. This is true especially of the sparrow.

The appearance of the marshes and other open surfaces is the most wintry at this season and remains so until spring is well started. Their herbage and other low growth is the first to wither or die. There is little, if anything, to relieve the pale, somber browns of shriveled leaves and stalks and the grayish dun of bare spaces. The hardy life of ducks, hawks, crows, and killdeers, with widespread invasions of grackles and other blackbirds, fixes the aspect of their haunts as one appropriate to winter. The marshes are naturally the coldest places in the coast district in winter. On the very rare occasions when their waters freeze over, ducks are in unmistakable difficulties. I came across such a situation once in the central part of the Louisiana coastlands. The early morning temperature had been about fifteen degrees. Many of the birds had come to a partly reclaimed savanna, where they found shallow holes thawed out with the first few hours of sunshine. Even ditches, sheltered from the hard north wind by the evergreen myrtles, yaupons, and small live oaks on their banks and, therefore, not freezing as heavily as more open waters, attracted some of the birds after the ice had melted.

Mild, clear weather is likely to hover over the low-lands at the turn of the year. Since a form of spring, not only in temperatures but in the state of vegetation, will follow within another six weeks, any indication of vernal conditions takes on a possibly undeserved significance, for in some ways the winter lies more ahead than behind. It is hard to ignore, however, the swelling flower buds of elm, the flowering of maple and cypress, and the promptness with which some herbage comes out in a week or so of springlike weather. There is even courtship among house sparrows this early, which of course is a matter of adaptation to the far southern weather by this alien species not shared by the native bird life except in a very few cases, notably the mating of the woodcock. This species must nest at least as early in some cases as the latter part of December, as young have been found a month later. The voices of frogs, which are lacking in Louisiana swamps only on cold nights, and the calls of tree toads are equal almost to their summer performances in a warm

[63]

rainy spell in early January or when mild, settled days have followed colder rains. Snakes are less prone to come out of their semi-hibernation until there is a longer sequence of warm days.

Symptoms of bird migration are not obvious until the end of January or beginning of February. Tree swallows increase over the numbers that have been about irregularly during the preceding part of the winter. Myrtle warblers become more numerous usually, apparently as the result of arrivals from farther south. Such northward trends of birds with a principally tropical distribution in winter may coincide with the coming of more northern species forced southward by cumulative effects of cold and reaching the coastlands just when a kind of simulated spring there would seem to contribute to their travel in the direction opposite to that from which they have come.

Traditional uncertainty of weather after the beginning of February borders on the fanciful in the coast region. Moderate cold is always to be expected, but the extremes have ranged from a month all spring to one involving most or all of the winter's abnormally cold days and more snow than it would be likely to have again in almost a century. The range of temperature is not greater, perhaps, than at higher latitudes but derives its peculiarity from the conversion of a land enjoying repeated equivalents of summer into one paralyzed by cold. As the dreaded intruder that lurks behind the mask of beguiling weather and nature's general clemency in the carnival season, one of these blizzard-like spells is a memory clearer to many than the normal rôle of February in the course of the Gulf Coast spring. It is undoubtedly disturbing to come out of swamps and woods bright with many indications of a returning reign of profusion or to watch the responses of gardens to the advancing tide of the year and then, within a day, to have it all obscured or even destroyed. Native growths, however, seldom, if ever, reach a point of development ahead of their power to resist the blighting effects of cold, which has only a retarding influence on their progress towards perfection. Leaves of live oak and magnolia were killed once in southern Louisiana by a temperature slightly above zero, but these trees did not fail to put out their usual growth of new leaves later in the spring. There was only a forcible shedding of the old ones before instead of after the appearance of the new ones.

As an aftermath of the widespread intensity of cold in the year 1899, ice floated down the Mississippi almost if not quite to the Gulf. This had no bearing, of course, on the local weather conditions. When the cold was present, the river was the usual rolling flood, but when the ice went past New Orleans, spring was beyond the point at which it could be menaced seriously. There they were, however, little white floes, or icebergs, drawn on by the inexorable current, while the green of willows and other hardy vegetation appeared freely over shores and levees. Probably no greater apparent contrast of seasons was ever known in this part of the world.

The most affirmative part of spring trends in February is the possible arrival after the middle of the month of at least three species of summer birds. The purple martin, the parula warbler, and the sycamore warbler come regularly or occasionally at this time. The martin is the most consistent in this respect. In advanced seasons, one may appear even in the first week of the month, though in recent years, such early arrival has been exceptional. It is not very unusual, however, for this species to be represented by bolder scouts by St. Valentine's Day. More come towards the end of the month or in the first few days of March. The parula warbler never returns quite this early unless conditions are much ahead of the average. The earliest arrival of this species of which there is a record is February 22. The sycamore warbler has almost identical migration habits in spring and has come at least by February 27. On the whole, it may be noted, the progress of spring has been considerably slower in recent years. Since the early part of the present century there have been few instances of advanced seasons.

The fresh, delicate brightness of the parula warbler or other forerunners of returning warmth and fullness of verdure is one of the special characteristics in the outdoor calendar of the lowlands. In the tasseling or spare leafage of willows, cypresses and live oaks, they are significant beyond comparison with their size and prominence, tokens of persistent revival of the color and richness of life.

Chilliness, drouth, or lack of sunshine in March can cause setbacks to the rising surge of spring, which may not overcome all obstacles until the equinoctial date. In between are passages of warmth and brightness that leave no doubt of the deep, pulsing flood of vitality, richness, and delicacy to come. Suddenly, at the end of March, the curtains of uncertainty are drawn aside to display the luxuriance of new leafy textures. Shades of green and effects of light and space that are forgotten from season to season have come back to the crowns and girths of elms, oaks, hackberries, and other ample-foliaged trees. The flow of life brings to the recesses of verdure such returning birds as vireos and orchard orioles. From this time on there can be no halting, nothing more than a deviation in forward movements of the season.

April days are crowded with unfolding events of plant and animal life. Trees of every kind reach a flush leafiness, most of the year's blossoming of woodland shrubs is under way or completed, and the birds are in bursting impulses of migration or nesting. Warm, showery weather halts some of their singing and showy activity but makes woods and groves the stage of an inquisitive, bewildering agility of warblers and other small, insectivorous, migratory species. They move in and out of the finer sprays of foliage and flit loosely and momentarily about their tips.

Full, white clouds float high and the assuring pungency of summer warmth is in the air on clear, lightly breezy days in April. A strain of indolence sounds in some of the bird notes, there is less restlessness among birds newly arrived. Shadows beneath the trees have become sharper, deep, luxuriant entrenchment of the influences of spring is everywhere, its surest single sign a richly golden butterfly, the tiger swallowtail, in strong, buoyant, yet drifting flight, among scattered trees or at the edge of the woods. These and many other things signalize the first meeting of the freshness of spring and the opulence of summer.

The last of spotless spring days are usually in the final week or so of April, a time when the substance and color of foliage have not lost any of their delicacy. Aftermath of thunder storms or other disturbances, they have a smooth vibrance of hue and atmospheric quality. Nothing is lacking to perfect them, nothing out of place. Light plays equally on every surface, a transparent brilliance spreads to water, trees, and sky. Swallows skim effortlessly in all directions, vivid orioles, buntings, and tanagers move among conspicuous trees, small, sharply active, minutely marked, and brightly colored warblers dip into and out of the foreground of foliage or slip into the depths of shiny green.

After variable weather in May, full-blown summer comes upon the coastlands in a setting of fervidly blue sky and heavy shadows blotched against the brilliance of sunlight and is keyed with the full-throated notes of nesting birds and the long, strident cadences of the tree-haunting "locusts." Successive increments of saturating sunshine and intensity of color follow the first realization of summer through quiet June days, especially after rainy spells. Fresh mornings and wet, steamy, or hot and glaring days, with balmy, often very beautiful nights, are the principal weather peculiarities past summer's turning point.

In this latitude, much vegetation, instead of being in its prime at the time of the solstice, as in more northern regions, has reached or gone beyond its maturity. The period of heat is not half gone, but for many plants growth is more than half completed and in some cases is practically at a standstill. Although for many weeks the superficial appearances are those of summer, hidden processes of life are pointing towards the quiescence of fall. Hot, dry days of July and much of August, even though interspersed in some years with many rains, are a time of stagnation for some birds and other life that ushered in the earliest warm days of spring.

Sometimes the greatest heat of the year accompanies the gradual disintegration of the summer pictures, with their ripening of all growths, the vanishing of some bird life, and the coming of early autumnal birds and flowers. Insect life, reinforced by the multiplied generations of the summer, has reached its highest pitch. One of nature's most remarkable pageants is in progress, but it passes so slowly that only the first distinct outline of approaching fall verifies the changes that have taken place.

CHAPTER VIII

Sure Strongholds of Birds

EXPLORATION OF SWAMPS and other woodland in coastal Louisiana leads to lasting acquaintance with much of its distinctive and attractive bird life. A little-frequented bayou or canal is sometimes the best approach to retreats of the more retiring birds. However reached, half-lighted cypress brakes, deeply thatched chambers and corridors of ripe, moist hardwood forests, and low, wet thickets of willows, buttonbushes, and clambering vines are the goals of search for such occupants. Visits to these segments of sunken, verdure-crowded expanses that make up much of lower Louisiana will reveal the greater part of its nesting bird life in full possession. The discoveries will be surprising not because they disclose birds unknown elsewhere but by showing them sometimes in exceptional abundance and in unique relationship with each other and with their environment.

Wherever the tangle is deep or the trees low, the white-eyed vireo is the inevitable and effervescent representative of birds that live freely and fruitfully in the richness of the swamp growth. Its short, vigorous song, variations of a general theme, "whit-tee—tee-ree-wee," lengthens into a chain of sounds that whips back and forth through the level, green spaces. Impressions of the exotic nature of the swamp come from the flashing colors and sprightly movements of the prothonotary warbler, which are more convincing than its lightly delivered song. It appears suddenly in a gap of the foliage as an excited fragment of golden, white, and blue feathers. For a moment or so it rests on a stump or dead branch, apparently unsettled on its next move. If it does not fly almost immediately, it droops its wings and tail and, raising and drawing in its head only slightly, lets slip from its throat a careless, unmodulated trill that has neither prelude nor flourish at the end but is just a fluid succession of whistling or clearly respired notes echoing among the walls of green. It leaves as hurriedly as it came, emphasizing its departure with a reverberating "twink." Somewhere near, in a low cavity of rotting ash, maple, or willow and probably over shallow water, the delicately marked eggs rest on a flimsy cushion of moss, small leaves, and shreds of other vegetation.

In parts of the swampier forest where cypress still grows in some abundance and where stretches of shallow water make ragged gaps among the trees there are sites suitable for the nesting of several of the larger water birds. It quickens interest after time spent among the small recluses of the swamps to come across anhingas, or water turkeys, and colonies or scattered individuals of herons in such places. Nearness to points of concentration for these species becomes evident with the opening of the view and the appearance well above the treetops of an occasional soaring water turkey or of herons bound towards or away from the gathering places. The herons, with their slow, rhythmic wing-beats and steadied courses, leave an impression of unfailing continuance of their life processes. Feeding themselves and their young, they have a day-long occupation of going and coming between the spots selected for the best protection of the nests and others supplying the greatest abundance of food.

The green heron is an independent member of the heron assemblages and does not confine itself to the immediate neighborhood of the rookeries; it is seldom gregarious, in fact, even with others of its species. One of these birds is a suddenly but not very frequently appearing figure at almost any point in the wetter woods. It rises abruptly from a slough with gangling, slouchy flight and hoarse whistling to post itself on a branch midway in a low tree. It stoops or crouches slightly, turning its head one way or another for a better view. If pressed too closely, it launches again in ungainly, swinging flight and makes off with various croaks and whistles. Sometimes in its place, the yellow-crowned night heron, the "grosbec" of the lowlands, will project itself into view under similar circumstances. When the green heron frequents the immediate neighborhood of the heron colonies it keeps generally to their outskirts, but the night heron mingles more closely and in greater numbers.

The principal beauty of the heron colony before hatching has begun and while the females are on the nests is the spectacle of male birds perched in various positions and at different heights in the cypresses and other trees, forming a kind of frieze. Both sexes are less absorbed in foraging than at a later stage of nesting. With heads drawn in between the shoulders, the birds sit mutely, stolidly above the feathery sprays of the cypresses, like graven images pledged to the inertness of the swamp.

The composition of heronries in the wooded swamps is in varying proportions of the large white, or American, egrets and little blue and yellow-crowned night herons, though there are colonies almost exclusively of one species. The rare snowy heron and the great blue heron have typical places in or about the colony. If it adjoins a marsh, there may be Louisiana herons. Altogether, the little blue heron outnumbers other species. Its color will not always identify it, as there is a phase of plumage, generally conceded to be that of immature birds only, in which it is entirely white. Other birds are mottled white and slaty blue. The purely white birds resemble the snowy heron, which is distinguished by its black bill and the black legs and yellow feet or, in more scientific terminology, the black tarsi ("legs") and yellow toes ("feet"). This is a better mark of identification than the plumes of the back, which are characteristic only of the female in the breeding season.

Ibises are among the rarer birds of true swamplands. Their retreats are most likely to be about the borders of secluded lakes or sloughs. Their habitats are contracting gradually, and it is an event of some importance to come across them, whether they be the once common white ibis, familiar in the swamp regions as a "beccroche," or "Spanish curlew," or the glossy ibis, which has never been plentiful. A very large swamp bird, member of the stork family but given the misnomer of wood ibis, is a fine figure and still of rather dependable occurrence in the wooded morasses or partly marshy districts near the coast. High over its haunts, circling powerfully and steadily, it is an astonishing example of bird life, with a wing expanse of about six feet. Like the white pelican and the whooping crane, it is entirely white except for the black wing tips.

Observation of a representative variety of birds in the lowlands is easiest in the rich woodlands that cover formerly submerged or very swampy surfaces of lower Louisiana. The transformation may have come about through the closing of crevasses or incidental effects of drainage in some other area. A beautiful forest having some of the appearances of lowland wet woods and of bottom lands at a higher level becomes the resort of many woodland birds. At some points it is sure to border more open situations as well as wet tangles and is thus within the range of the fullest variety of bird life. Woods like these are green from the floor to the crown in the warmer months. Wild cane, creeping grasses, succulent herbs, and trailing or climbing vines fill out much of the lower spaces, but there is no jungle-like aspect, as in the lowest swamps. Sweet gums, elms, and water oaks rise everywhere to impressive heights, making room below for maples, honey locusts, haws, and other low trees. Ash, sycamore, and hackberry are important also in the make-up of this forest, in which grow altogether about twenty-five species of trees, including live oak on the slight elevations and cypress and tupelo on the damper sites.

In growths of the kind just described, a lover of woodlands will find combined the luxuriance of lowland vegetation and things pertaining to a seasoned forest in a final expression of sylvan seclusion. Nature has made a stand in the undisturbed disposition of her riches here and fixed provisions for quiet sequence of life and growth. Birds move about almost sedately; a strange secrecy covers the life of thrushes, vireos, warblers, and other woodland kinds; their voices advance and recede deceptively among leafy masses. An atten-

tive listener will catch the leisurely, almost question-
ing notes of the summer tanager, pitched to the meas-
ure of light, breezy motions in the highest sprays. The
hooded warbler, concealed in the heavy leafage and
singing from a lower level, flings the wild, rounded
syllables of its brief, unhesitant song into the circle of
echoing voices. White-eyed vireos, constant vocalists
of all lowland woods, wet or merely moist, supply all
gaps in the chorus, most of them singing from the
lower trees or bushier woodland clumps.

The red-eyed vireo, keeping higher than its kin,
adds almost as persistently to the volume of notes in
these woods, but, with its far less sprightly and extended utterances, it attracts from a human listener
only a kind of subconscious attention. One knows always that it is about but would be willing occasionally
to forget its endlessly reiterated "whee-wee—whee-
wah." No such objection is made to the parula warbler's half-tone, buzzing little trill, which issues from
the denser foliage of moss-draped trees almost as
steadily as the sounds of insects in the fields. The little
blue and white singer, scantily marked with gold and
bronze on back and breast, discontinues its busy search
for insects only for as long as it takes to deliver the
peculiar, almost metallic-sounding fragment of harmony. The notes rise high enough in the nearest trees
to be heard plainly but drift in as a kind of whisper
from more distant ones.

Low, matted herbage covering the ground in the moister parts of the woods are irresistible for the shy Kentucky warbler, wearing a livery of pure green above and rich yellow below. It moves lightly on or near the ground, whence it delivers a short lay with a soft, ventriloqual quality so that it seems to travel from all parts of the woods. The sweet, light refrain of this little recluse is as pleasing as the mellowed richness of old forests.

Other birds have parts in the symphony of these retreats in the best days of spring and summer. Songs, calls, or twitterings of cardinals, wood thrushes, titmice, Carolina wrens, flycatchers, and cuckoos are seldom missing in the musical passages that ebb and flow on every hand. Strange figures and voices of kinds that react sensitively to changes of weather in the period of spring migration are present or absent with subtle uncertainty. Ovenbirds, cerulean warblers, redstarts, gray-cheeked thrushes, scarlet tanagers, and the rarer flycatchers invest the familiar haunts of more obvious species with a passing enchantment. After the brief presence of these evanescent pilgrims, the woods belong conclusively to the kinds that live in them with the confidence of a native's habituation.

CHAPTER IX

Profiles of Wood, Stream, and Shore

FOR A REGION with few elevations as much as fifty feet, the coast district in Louisiana and Mississippi, and especially in the former state, has an astonishing diversity of surfaces. In Louisiana, even the marshes, extending inland at most points for a distance of from fifteen to thirty miles from the irregular coast contour, have very changeable prospects. The Mississippi coast, rising immediately along most of its extent to an elevation seldom less than fifteen or twenty feet above ordinary tides, is much more uniform. The two states have a common type of coastal scenes in the immediate vicinity of Pearl River, which divides them and flows here virtually at tide level.

A general, though not always continuous, view of the surface in parts of the Louisiana coast district is possible only from some waterway, while in others, lakes and streams are merely features of the topography as seen from land on which there is a way to come and go. By the use of both land and water routes necessary for intimate acquaintance with the lowland area, there is full comprehension of its general peculiarity and flexible picturesqueness. Following only the waterways, an explorer or excursionist in the lowlands misses the contrasts or at least comes upon them so gradually as to see them to less advantage, while no road nor path over traversable land can reach certain inner scenes of the marsh and swamp. Sudden disclosure of water, transitions from wooded to open views, and abrupt changes in growth are the principal variations on which the uniqueness of Louisiana coastal scenery turns.

Exactly what natural attractions are peculiar to the lowlands is not always obvious. They are certainly remarkable for the almost infinite designs of a generally similar pattern. Variety may seem unlikely in a flat country, but with water as a key to its formations and textures, there is hardly a limit to the kinds of scenes and conditions that take shape. There are fewer clearly and permanently distinct types of scenery than in a country of more irregular contours, but the unexpectedness of new outlooks is always interesting.

Tempting perspectives in the tidelands center on a mingling of salt marsh, plumy, island-like brakes of cypress, and scattered pines on a low savanna, all linked by the meanderings of a wide, gracefully turned bayou. With the briskness of the seashore, they border on the seclusion of inland streams and borrow the freshness of the prairies. Hints of bass, water birds, and forest game mingle in their diversity. Here, within a circle of fresh and brackish water, is a metropolis of boggy lands and sandy flats, pools where white water lilies float, others with yellow pond lilies, muddy banks of iris and spider lilies. Upstream are the first water margins and woodland edges that bring together in spring the golden-club, silver-bell, even the flowering dogwood.

The shores of Lake Pontchartrain are full of easy transformations in lowland scenery. The lake is adjacent to nearly every phase of the coast terrain except dry prairie lands. In reality, it is a landlocked bay rather than a lake, so that it has both a maritime and an inland character. Pines and stretches of richer forest are on its slightly elevated northern shore. Towards its eastern outlets a maze of tidal marshes, lagoons, and bayous draw away from the more open water to inland reaches, where there are insulated oaky ridges and very low pinewoods. The region bordering it on the south and west changes from one of brackish marshes near the outlets to fresh-water marsh and deeply swampy woods.

Beyond the western end of the lake is an almost primeval fastness of flooded growths of cypress and the trees that grow near or with it, the home of deer, alligators, great frogs, and herons, ibises, and other birds of the swamp. It is a mysterious maze of unmeasured currents and shallow swamp waters, palmetto and lotus, some remnant of the larger cypresses, and tangles of maple and ash brilliant in late winter and very early spring with their leaf-like flowers-parts.

The changing vistas and overlapping expanses are most striking on the northern shores of Lake Pontchartrain. At some places the pines reach nearly to the water, marking the beach as an outpost of contours that lift gradually inland. Flanking the piney space is sometimes a marshy cove, sometimes an open grove of small but old and somewhat battered live oaks, veterans that face the winds or tides, yet are set as if in retreat to the woodlands behind them, trees that hold the last claim of the forest in this sea-level country but post one of the surest signs of a shore ruled by the tide. The mosaic of effects possible is still greater about the estuaries of two rivers and the mouths of several bayous that enter Lake Pontchartrain from the north. Pines, marsh, widespread cypresses, and woodlands on the first rise of ground are a varied panel of heavy growth welded with the shadows of the quiet water.

Broad views that include tidal marshes and segments of the wooded swamp are finest to the east of New Orleans, in an area beginning on highway or railroad at about Micheaud and spreading eastward several miles beyond Pearl River. With a region to the south, made up almost exclusively of small bays, salt-water lakes, and marshy flats, it has the collective

designation of "Louisiana Marshes" and is the general
tidewater region east of the Mississippi. Its beauty and
diversity make it a remarkable panorama from the
travel axis that passes through it in a generally east
and west direction. Followed from New Orleans, the
route clears the nondescript outskirts of the city, truck
gardens, half-wild pastures, and low, ragged, half-
drained woods. After it has crossed the last small
waterway of the swamps, it emerges rather suddenly
into the sweep of marsh and a wheeling circumference
of watery and woodland hazes. The mustiness of the
city and the dullness of the first lands beyond it fall
away; for miles the view is a clear, breezy prospect,
with nothing but scattered hunting and fishing camps
to detract from the view, and even some of these are
picturesque. Little appears on the horizon but interrupted fringes of woods, the smoke of an invisible train,
or, across water, the outline of a boat.

At the bridge across the Rigolets—deep, tide-swept
pass between Lake Pontchartrain and Mississippi
Sound—a vastness of bright waters and variegated
marshy surface extends to a horizon either glittering
with the distant dancing of waves or traced in a splic-
ing of shores and ridges etched with live oak, pine, or
cypress. It is the crossing point of lines of vision that
lead to the many parts of this mutable domain.

Eastward from the Rigolets, which, curiously, is one
of the corporation limits of the City of New Orleans

though nearly thirty miles from the center of that community, lies the delta of Pearl River. It is not a muddy, treeless one, like that of the Mississippi, but an uncertain area of wet, lightly wooded tracts, narrow brakes of cypress, and even slight ridges of pine-bearing clay. The main stream and its branches are wider and somewhat less winding than most bayous of the cypress swamp districts. The principal body of the stream is a translucent, light mahogany color except in a flood stage. Its placid course is between clean shores sharply edged with short, slender rushes and grasses or past low, tawny banks overspread by large live oaks or by cypresses growing at the water's edge. The scene has a singularly bright and simple picturesqueness.

Out of the delta of Pearl River, the terrain changes within a brief space to the pine-forested coastal plateau of Mississippi, a country of white sand, red and yellow clays, and upland oaks, varied by sinks with a richer soil and more luxuriant trees, or by damp savannas among the pines. On the typical pine meadow there is a great variety of flowering herbs, including pitcher plant, meadow-beauty, Sabbatia, a flame-orange milkweed (*Asclepias paupercula*), Catesby lily, and the small blue iris. Their blooms dapple the grassy surface with a succession of conspicuous colors from early spring to mid-fall.

The contrasts of scenic elements are less numerous and more nearly fixed on the Mississippi coast than in

Louisiana. The strip of white sandy beach, most of it now behind a sea wall, and sharply defined growths of pine and oak that rise at once from its inner edge are the central pattern in a general prospect of the coast. An occasional depression edging back from the shore line makes a little bay of boggy ground and marshy growth, the haunt of fiddler crabs and suggestive of the odor of iodine. It lies like an amphitheater within the terrace of gum and sweet bay and pines that shoulder above it. Though slight in extent, such spots have a bold relief in the prevailing scene along the coast. A rill of amber-colored water is an uncertain outlet to the beach, for usually it ends in a sea wall, or tides and waves keep its mouth blocked with sand.

Several bays that enter the Mississippi coast are very important in diversifying its scenery. Like the outer coastline, their shores are occasionally marshy. Small rivers, issuing picturesquely from rising pinelands, mingle with the upper waters of the inlets in a vivid and complicated picture. It has the combined character of bayous, leafy screens of bottom growth, upland streams, and open pinewoods that fill out most of the distances. Its unfailing repose seems almost impossible so near the constantly restless seaside.

CHAPTER X

In an Overflow of Green

A NARROW FRINGE of habitable land on the west side of the Mississippi River below New Orleans is a picturesque concentration of the peculiar and intriguing Louisiana coast country. It is the core of Plaquemines parish, longest and narrowest of the subdivisions of Louisiana and the reversed funnel through which the great river finally works itself free from its vague and incoherent delta plain and, regaining momentum in the narrower channels and jettied passes, rolls out in a vast wall of fluid silt to meet the first green waters of the Gulf. Except for the seat of government, which is on the east side of the river, this flange of the parish has most of the distinctive and significant ingredients of life and appearance along the final reaches of the Mississippi. Even its climate is different, being perceptibly milder in winter, since the exposure is more nearly towards the Gulf. At the river's end there is no separation of east and west, for bays, marshes, mud flats, and stream merge in a panel of nearly indistinguishable parts only a few degrees removed from the uniformity of the sea. Everything, whether pilots' station, lighthouse, jetty works, duck club, or quarantine base, is across water in some direction from something else; that most of these landmarks are to the east of the main course of the stream is incidental.

Detached from New Orleans and other communities except for a lesser highway and a single-track, lightly ballasted railroad, which runs inconsequently beside the levee or among orange groves and across home sites, the segment of Plaquemines parish west of the river is an almost incredibly unique land. Its ribbon of usable and cultivable land even upstream is hardly a mile in width, and practically all of its inhabitants live within a few acres of the river. At any point, farming, dwelling, and transportation must meet their needs within this narrow strip, bound together like a braid of dissimilar cords, in a strange complex of settlement and natural surroundings, the artificial against a background of flat, fertile spaces that would be a wilderness of lowland growths if left to themselves. The knots of this strand come closer together with growing demands for reclamation of the potential wealth, but seldom do they grow larger except along one axis.

The population, natives and newcomers, probably the most mixed in racial strains to be found anywhere in the coast region outside of New Orleans, are singularly and almost unanimously absorbed in prospering from the products of water and soil. They have developed a phase of living that is at once distinctive and a dependable source of income at home and of appreciation abroad.

It is a paradox that as it nears its end, the Mississippi, greatest and in some ways most characteristic of North American rivers and in this part of its course a lane for ocean-going vessels, should border surroundings so unlike those by which it passes elsewhere. This section is peculiar, in fact, not only in its physical isolation but in the development it has undergone at the hands of man. Its extreme fertility and the mellowing influence of the warm, humid coast atmosphere have enabled its inhabitants to turn it into a kind of horticultural bower, screened in orange groves and decorative shrubs, quilted with market gardens and lily beds, and bordered by the low, willow-fringed levee at the front and scraggly, stunted, wet woodland or open marsh in the rear.

There are probably few localities or communities as highly developed agriculturally or horticulturally and at the same time as much cut off as these Plaquemines parish lands. They have all the appearance of a straggling, richly and closely planted village, the massed foliage of orange trees most in evidence. In spring they are alive with migratory birds and when these are gone, there is still a confident and numerous contingent of others, like the painted bunting, orchard oriole, cardinal, and mockingbird, to make the groves and thickets lively. Colors swim before the eye in the brilliant sunshine in which the land is immersed. No small fraction of the earth is unproductive of vegetation, and a low canopy of verdure spreads wherever human occupation will allow it. When rice was cultivated more widely than at present, the effect was even more striking. The unkempt sward of levees, ditch banks, roadside, lanes, and fringes of fields contributes almost as greatly to this brightness as the flush, green levels of the rice.

Though the Plaquemines parish orange country lacks approach by a main highway and remains essentially peculiar in its physical appearance, there is enough continuous coming and going on all accounts to take from it some of its striking quaintness. When its only assets were its damp, fertile soil, floods of sunshine, the rice and sugar-cane fields, a few orange trees, and nature's crops in the surrounding elements, caught or gathered in an unorganized way, it was a realm apart. It was neither countryside nor wilderness but a casual part of the lowland world. Complacent, sociably inclined Creoles and a few English-speaking families from elsewhere were its principal dwellers. Crops and storms, mosquitoes and subtropical rains, an informal little railroad train, and irregularly visited store or post office summed up for them an existence without much beginning or end.

[89]

Life in these surroundings rose seldom above the level of simple activities, an all-enveloping tranquillity, and an inert, inarticulate beauty stamped here by nature. Changelessness dwelt in the quiet and in the static hue of the rice fields; contradicting it was the swish against the foot of the levee from the wake of a steamer plodding ahead in midstream, strangely contrasting token of scenes far different from the lustrous and almost sumptuous complacency of the smoothly expanded prospect and the unconcerned provinciality that prospered in its midst.

There was variation from the passivity of this environment for one who found interest and pleasure in the ubiquitous bird life. It was even more abundant then than now, especially the kinds attracted to the rice fields, and presented constantly new fronts. Along the levee and the roadside and in the trees about the homes the scene was a fragment of better known rural settings, where a few of the more familiar kinds afforded at least a reflection of bird life in other farming and plantation country. Just beyond lay the seclusion of the rice fields, in which furtive king rails and purple gallinules held hidden conclaves in the tunneled thatch of the stalks and the rank depths of wild coffee and indigo and water plants along the ditches or small canals. If a hunter invaded the cover in which they live, he might flush one here and there, but oftener than not the bird would rise at a moment when the hunter had plunged into a high growth, obstructing his view, or was struggling for a foothold in the uncertainties of the flooded ground. Thus many of the apparently easy opportunities of bagging one of the indifferently regarded game birds were lost. A chance to see how well they protected themselves in these splashy, soggy, thickly sown grounds was a spectacle well worth the floundering progress in their haunts.

At threshing time the rice fields took on another aspect of their attractiveness for birds. There was a thronging commotion that did not belong with the constancy of summer quietude. Occasional bobolinks in their subdued autumn dress, joined by the little sora rails, arrived in the van of the fall migration. It was the season of greatest hubbub and activity in these lands. Boys with guns, long, cracking whips, and even sticks took stands about the fields to keep away the blackbirds and even to turn their attention to throwing the sticks at the weak-flighted rails that rose ahead of the threshers, expertly enough at times to vindicate this peculiar style of bagging the small game birds.

The end of the rice-harvesting season shifted the outlook to other mild excitements among the dwellers of this country. Gathering of pecans, visits of city hunters when ducks and snipe should become plentiful, and the cutting of sugar cane and picking of the orange crop were the next expectations. The mental weather had had its principal change of the year, but until another rice crop was in the making, the seasons would shift at an incalculably slower pace.

CHAPTER XI

An Ornithologist in the City

ENOUGH BIRDS to whet the interest of an observer are present sometimes in a large city and especially in its suburbs. There was a time when New Orleans was sufficiently favored in this respect to keep alive the keen zest of early ornithological studies. Some parts of it were almost like the country, and neighborhoods far within the city proper were at least visiting grounds for unexpected birds. Glimpses of these strangers were like being transported suddenly to their mystifying haunts in the woods. While some of the commoner birds, as jays, robins, mockingbirds, grackles, and orchard orioles, continue numerous and others, although not well adapted to modern urban conditions, still appear occasionally in the city, enjoyment of the more unusual phases of bird life there is largely one of reminiscence.

Even formerly nothing would have seemed more improbable to the uninitiated than the occurrence of certain birds in the city and the circumstances under which they came there. Once, when my interest in ornithology was in the formative stage, I had a mingled feeling of curiosity in something new to me and of reproach for a boy who had shot a very small bird from a bare tallow-tree [1] in an old and closely built neighborhood. I had no idea of its identity but marveled at its extremely diminutive size, which was not much greater from tip to tip than that of a hummingbird and represented a not much greater bulk. Equally astonishing was its clear olive green plumage above, almost like a bright dye. It impressed me as just a mite that had drifted into the bare precincts of walls and pavements, wires and street rails, where trees struggled but seldom prospered and where, on a gray winter day, it had met its end through the thoughtlessness of one boy and had contributed a new glimpse of strange horizons to another. As I realized later, it was a kinglet, the ruby-crowned, though in the plumage of this particular individual, the distinctive head marking was lacking. A third boy who happened along at the time identified it as a "milk bird," which display of knowledge brought to my mind some crude and indefinite associations but did not appeal very much to my instinctive sense of the fitness of nature. Did it exude milk like the stems of certain juicy plants, or did it extract the fluid from some mysterious source? These profound speculations must have been sufficient at

[1] *Sapium sebiferum,* an introduced Chinese tree of the spurge family.

least to spur me on to a greater desire to fathom the strangeness of the feathered world.

Some spots about the city, of course, were more attractive to birds than others. One, known as "Blue Alley," in an uptown neighborhood, had a rare touch of wildness for a metropolitan area. It was the unusual combination of an uncovered drainage canal, an impenetrable hedge of "Cherokee" rose that flanked the canal on one side, and a pathway beneath a row of Osage-orange trees that ran on the other. Although it was within close reach of buildings and sounds of the city, it was as little visited as a country lane. Such a place, when interesting phases of migration were in progress and a trip into the country was impossible, was a partial compensation for a bird-lover confined to the city. In this strange recess the writer and fellow bird-students saw at various times such birds, rather uncommon in Louisiana, as the ovenbird, purple finch, white-crowned sparrow, and Philadelphia vireo. A good many other interesting species were almost always certain to be there in the migration periods.

Followed far enough, "Blue Alley" ceased to be a hybrid between an embryonic city street and a rural byway and led on to the unfenced pasturage that spread behind the upper section of the city. The latter was merely a muddy or grassy waste on which palmettos still grew and over which dairy cattle of a sort grazed more or less freely. A few hunters went there at the right seasons for an occasional chance to shoot jacksnipe and upland plovers. Great flocks of pipits, little brownish, ground-loving birds with streaked breasts, came to the better grazed pastures in winter, and savanna sparrows, the "ground sparrows" of boy hunters in those days of unregulated shooting, were common enough in the short grass or on the bare earth of what had been kitchen garden patches of the preceding summer. Otherwise, bird life of the "commons" was usually rather limited.

When most of Audubon Park was a great meadow bedded deep with white and pink clover in spring and early summer, it was a haunt of the grasshopper sparrow. At least one of these diminutive birds, perched on a thistle or other coarse weed, was in sight in any patch of a few acres. The chirping, insect-like notes that give it its name were not hard to detect after a little acquaintance with the singer. The conversion of the open parts of the park into golf links or regularly mowed hayfields put an end to the grasshopper sparrows, which have become something of a rarity even in country fields.

With the grasshopper sparrow, especially in late spring, was the black-throated bunting, or dickcissel, but the association was incidental. The sparrows were in the clover, low weeds, and other herbage, the buntings posted on scattered saplings and tall weeds, from which they delivered their odd ditties across the spaces of these old plantation and exposition grounds, producing the effect of a number of little trip hammers striking in unison, slowing down frequently to individual performances. The days of this rather inharmonious concert were over soon, and only a pair or so of the birds remained to nest near the little neglected lake where once Pompeii had fallen as part of a fireworks program.

The rain-crow, or yellow-billed cuckoo, was an intriguing bird figure in shady yards in summer. It might be more correct to say that it was a bird phantom. Its almost uncanny concealment in the foliage of tall trees while it paid off its slowly croaking, unbirdlike notes in an atmosphere of humid warmth to the accompaniment of drowsing insect sounds, brought a touch of exotic sloth to the quality of sunny, stagnant days. It was an incarnation of tropic influences and its life more like the sluggishness of cold-blooded vertebrates than the animation of feathered life. On breezier days or when the air was lighter or showers fell, its activity was greater, and increased the chances of seeing its pliant, sweeping form on the way between trees.

The myrtle, or yellow-rumped, warbler was once the commonest native bird in New Orleans in winter. It was known under the colloquial name of "teteet," traceable to the local French habit of identifying and lumping together most of the less readily recognized small birds as "petites." To English-speaking boys and some adults, birds so named became "teteets," or even "teteeses," apparently by a kind of alliteration. These little birds were everywhere in garden or sidewalk trees and shrubbery.

While cardinals are fully as numerous in New Orleans now as they were formerly, the appearance of tanagers in the city has become as rare as that of some of the large and small birds in the wilds. Some years ago it was not unusual to see them during both the spring and the fall migrations. A young friend and I had our first look at scarlet tanagers not in the woods but in New Orleans. Standing on an upstairs porch, we happened to look at a giant water oak in the fine grounds of a neighbor in one of the older residential sections, even then well towards the heart of the city. The tree was freshly green in the perfect weather of mid-April, and to our amazement we discovered that its ample branches and foliage were full of flaming red birds, a score or more. With the help of a pair of opera glasses, which we passed grudgingly back and forth, we established that the birds were tanagers, about equally divided between the two species, the summer and the scarlet. My friend was a guest for Sunday dinner, but my recollection is that we could not get our minds off the birds long enough to take much interest in the meal. Newcomers in the field of bird study, we had seen almost as many tanagers in one tree as if they had been blackbirds or robins. The reason for the presence of so many of the birds in a single tree, even though a large one, must have been an abundance of some particular insect that they relished. Rarely do more than two or three of them appear together.

The yellow warbler, or summer yellowbird, is another species that practically has disappeared from the New Orleans scene and has become far less common also in all of southern Louisiana and Mississippi and probably most parts of the country. Its appearance in New Orleans was under peculiar circumstances. While some pass northward through this region in April as transients that breed somewhat beyond the coastal strip, these or others are back again on their southward migration as early as the second week in July. Thus, some of them are, or were, present for the greater part of the summer. At one time, on hot, bright mornings after July 15, the air at heights varying from two hundred feet to two hundred yards was full of the returned or returning migrants. Their thin "zits" could be heard continually, but their small, slender forms, silhouetted like small darts of incandescent gold against the sky, were not always easily discernible. On the edge of town it was easier to see them, as they came down to weedy lots or fields, and were especially plentiful in the giant ragweeds. There was no bird more characteristic of the ardent summer days.

After the fall equinox, indigo buntings and Tennessee warblers took the place of yellow warblers in the air over the more open parts of the city. Nearly all of the buntings were in the plain, brownish plumage distinctive at other seasons of the female and of all immature birds. They passed overhead in their migratory restlessness, going from one outskirt to another, thus making some progress in their travels by day as well as by night. The sharp "tzeet" of the indigo bunting and the light "tsit" of the Tennessee warbler were almost incessant on bright days in late September and early October. A few of them came down at favorable points, but most were on their way to the open countryside over which they spread at times in remarkable numbers. Except when so plentiful, the Tennessee warbler would attract little attention if one were not on the lookout for it. It is one of the smaller warblers and its markings of green, greenish yellow, and grayish white are inconspicuous.

One fall a remarkable migration of small birds passed through New Orleans. Observed in a neighborhood near Audubon Park, the display lasted five days, beginning October 7, which was overcast and a little cooler than preceding days. Birds were not merely plentiful but present in overflowing abundance in the trees and garden shrubbery. Rarely, if ever, have I seen together as many different kinds in as great numbers. Repeatedly I saw three or four summer tanagers in a single tree. Wood pewees were even more plentiful, appropriating almost every available exposed

perch. Unusual restlessness for this species and repeated calls made them very conspicuous. As many as
four or five magnolia warblers appeared in some of the
small trees. Male scarlet tanagers, in the peculiar autumn plumage, in which a bright canary or almost
orange yellow replaces the scarlet of spring and summer, with the wings and tail remaining black, were in
the throng of migrants. White-eyed vireos were commoner than I have ever known them in the swamps
during the summer. Altogether about thirty species,
including the Philadelphia vireo and several of the less
common warblers, were present within an area of a
few squares.

Before the invasion was over I had one opportunity
to get to the nearest extensive woods. While I saw
small birds, especially Tennessee warblers, in almost
incredible numbers, mosquitoes were so bad and birds,
particularly the various wood warblers, were so often
in the taller trees and kept moving so constantly, that
it was impossible to follow enough of them closely with
the eye to form a satisfactory idea of the composition
of this great migratory bird host. Undoubtedly the
majority of them would have proved to be of the same
species as those already observed under more favorable circumstances, but certainly among so many birds,
there must have been some that would be accounted
rare in the Louisiana lowlands.

As a contrast to the lingering of fall migrants, the

quick passage of rare spring birds, all intensity, bright colors, and strong movement, that appeared sometimes in suburban neighborhoods was memorable. An array of this kind appeared on April 21 one year in the neighborhood to which I have referred. It was a day of singular brightness and mild crispness after slight cyclonic disturbances. It brought Baltimore oriole, rosebreasted grosbeak, scarlet tanager. The warblers identified numbered fourteen species. Fifty species in all, some not migratory, of course, came under my observation. By making a brief visit to a point across the Mississippi, I saw about twenty-five others. The growing rarity of many species of American birds and the increasingly unfavorable conditions in and about most large cities have made impossible such an opportunity for observation of birds in an urban area, although it is still to be found elsewhere.

CHAPTER XII

Intrusion of the Sea

IN BRIGHT WEATHER, tide-level reaches of the Louisiana coast have the character of land, however tenuous, but menacing, whipping winds, scudding clouds, and gusty rains take them over as a province of the sea. The marsh grasses and rushes and the last clumps of reeds lose their office as products of the shore and fade into the general grayness and loosening of the elements. All the seemingly ordered balance of the two realms collapses, and everything definite goes adrift in the wildness of shifting forces from the unhemmed spaces of water and sky. The little lagoons that had an individuality among the rushy spaces, the bright margins setting a division between water and vegetation, and the delineation of bayous tracing distinct paths across an all but aqueous world have become merged in an overwhelming ascendancy of the sea. The gray gulf, spits and bars awash, and the tide-level marsh are all one. In the welter of rain and waves and spray, nothing contradictory of the sea is in sight. Nowhere in the marsh is there anything with an appearance of permanence.

With stormy air and mounting tides, the wildness of the coast and the wastes of low vegetation are congenial to no life but the hardiest water birds, but in them it creates greater restlessness and boldness. As the pall of driving rain and gathering waves brings beach, flats, bars, and inlets into its compass and makes them all a bare stage for sea strength at play, gulls rise to meet the buffeting, call wildly, become newly vital in the surrounding chaos. The pelting of wind and water sweep the coastal reaches until retreat or resistance is the only way for birds that haunt these spaces undisturbed in the calmer days. Now the scene, leaden and shelterless, is full of hurrying forms, banks of clouds, and squally rains.

Pelicans are strong figures in the presence of the storm, now dominating every visible expanse of merging sea and sky, with its winds, its waves, and its gray and white clouds and rain. Though bulky and slow, these birds are able to withstand the rougher days of the coast and, like stout ships, ride out the gale. If disposed to fly, they are always able to trim a course that appears never in danger of being broken. In the heaviest blows the pelican flies near the water and proceeds with tireless regularity. Such flight replaces entirely the higher circling and cruising seen in fair weather. The rain is of even less effect than the wind on the strength and composure of one of these birds. Resting on the water or protruding surfaces, such as parts of an island or point that stay above most storm tides, it keeps its usual, unhuddled posture. Not only is it waterproof but seemingly insensible to the force of rains that would make most birds recoil.

Against the background of the gale and the deluge, birds of the seashore seem ever on the point either of venturing out into its farthest reaches or of bringing with them a message of the untamed sea. Gulls, solitary, in little squads, or in scattering banks, stand off vaguely in the vapory distance, beat desperately against the wind without ever faltering entirely, find a new tack, then sail or drift closer to the edges of the marsh and the resting spots now all but covered with water. Doubtless, like the other sea birds, they would not seek the storm, since it interferes with their feeding, but once caught in it they are capable of combating it. Dependent at all times on a strong, wandering flight to keep up with the shifting presence of fish, shrimp, or other sea creatures on which they exist, they have no less incentive to rove along the coast in a stormy atmosphere. If they could escape the grip of the gale and find quieter waters where their prey would be present, undoubtedly they would do it. When the storm is long continued, this is what many of them manage eventually to do. At first, however, their movements, especially those of the gulls, are wild, restless, and confused. The Caspian and royal terns appear to have as strong flight as the gulls, but, even with allowance for their fewer numbers, they are decidedly less conspicuous than the gulls in these times. Their flight is more rapid and direct than that of gulls and their general habits of life are more consistent, and it may be that many of them draw away from the storm area at the outset. Smaller terns, especially the least and Forster's, are inclined to move inland even in good summer weather, and few of them are over the open Gulf in a time of disturbance. They are not unequal, however, to keeping awing in almost the heaviest gale.

If the stormy days are in late summer or early fall, the man-of-war bird is conspicuous. As it braves the power of wind and sea, it has a spectacular part in the maneuvers of feathered mariners. A dark, gaunt form —large, powerful, unintimidated, and of almost sinister appearance—it comes into the center of the storm, swaying, sailing, or poising for a new slant but keeping steadily in flight. It does not go as high aloft, of course, as in fine weather, but it is still the intrepid courser of the air. Only the worst hurricane can compel it at times to come to rest on a seacoast structure or to go inland for the purpose of finding a place to light. As far as the writer knows, it never rests on the water. The remarkable strength of its wings, which spread at least seven feet, is offset by the smallness and weakness of the feet, so that it is unable to swim and for the same reason is not a diver. The whole economy of the man-of-war bird's life rests on its extraordinary aerial performances, which it uses to good effect in swooping at gulls and terns on the wing and either seizing from them their catches of fish before they can be disposed of or picking the prey from the air after the original and bewildered captor drops it.

In contrast to the response of pelicans, gulls, and man-of-war birds to the onslaughts of coast storms, the behavior of the shore birds is one of dispersion. Huddled on a beach or flying close to the water at their highest speed, the sandpipers and small plovers, little gray and flashing white figures, are mere futile-seeming wisps in the dull silvery rain and spray. Willets, curlews, oyster-catchers, and the larger plovers are more suited, at least in appearance, to the stresses of their surroundings. When circumstances compel them to move away, they have still the confidence and directness of flight that distinguish them at other times.

The life of birds characteristic of the tide marshes suffers an eclipse in the presence of storms. Only the clapper rail, most aquatic of this company, carries on an existence most nearly like that to which it is accustomed when the coast reposes in an even tenor of tides, winds, clouds, and sunshine. It either stays close in the best available cover of the marsh or skulks hurriedly about more open places in search for better shelter. Seaside sparrows, red-winged blackbirds, boat-tailed grackles, and marsh wrens either find protection where they are or move into less exposed areas. When the storm is over, they soon reassemble, to lead their freer and more prosperous life in an environment in which both the sea and traces of land are parts.

CHAPTER ·XIII

Domain of the Snipe

THE LIFE of the jacksnipe in Louisiana lowlands is convincing proof that there is an enduring haven for some of the wilder birds in these level, intractable expanses. The unrolling, immeasurable extent of cushiony sequences comes alive with an invasion of snipe. Buoyant and vigorous, these birds make it their own in a way more striking than in the case of any other species. They extract every last benefit from it and find in its enforcement of immobility on so many other creatures an actual provocation for their changeful, overflowing quickness and energy. As impetuous, unpredictable dwellers in the fastness of the wet lands, they come in remarkable numbers in fall, winter, and early spring. The grounds attracting them are so widespread and varied, and the birds themselves so erratic, sensitive, and volatile that fluctuations in their numbers and dispersion take place with startling rapidity.

A change in winds, tides, temperature, and possibly unknown factors may bring snipe or dislodge them overnight in a particular locality. They are in constant shift among water-dappled flats, rice lands, wet prairies, and rain-flooded fields and pastures. The temporary profusion of the birds in marshes of a certain type or in other wet ground may mean unbounded enthusiasm or complete confusion of a hunter. Sometimes they are so nervous and fugitive that no strategy will keep them from rising out of range, one after another, with discouraging regularity.

Under average circumstances, there are always snipe from October to March, and even April, in boggy stretches scantily covered with short grass and other low growths that do not interfere with the birds' resting on the mud and probing there for small, concealed organisms, such as worms and the lesser mollusks and crustaceans, and moving freely in any direction when they choose. Unless the wind is high and unless approached too closely, the snipe relies largely on crouching in such surroundings as a means of escape. If it does fly when there is no wind, it starts with twisting movements away from the hunter and then moves more directly. At other times it has to steady itself in the teeth of the wind, which it breasts before going with it, and so must take flight sooner. On a quiet day, therefore, a hunter who fails to bag snipe blames his markmanship rather than the lack of opportunities for a shot. The birds may be wary, of course, from continuous shooting on the same grounds. If the feeding as well as weather conditions are right for the purpose, a hunter on coast grounds commonly suited to snipe rarely fails to find the interest and success that go with the pursuit of these mettlesome birds. Though generally distributed over the lowlands, they are most plentiful in the central and western areas of the coast belt.

Snipe and duck haunts in the wild, marshy lands of Louisiana complement each other. Snipe go where there is only muck or too little water to attract many ducks, and wherever ducks feed they prefer the shelter of the taller growths of the marsh. Snipe can hide in the shortest grass or in the withered vestiges of marsh herbage. Sometimes the snipe find congenial places at the edges of small water holes among the sheltering vegetation. Ducks are hunted in Louisiana usually from water blinds reached by pirogues, while snipe, of course, are hunted on foot, and so duck hunters and snipe hunters are rarely in actual contact. Duck hunting necessitates transit over watery tracts and surfaces of the marsh, while snipe hunting depends on walking over its less treacherous expanses.

The effect of windy weather on the outcome of snipe hunting is entirely different from that on duck hunting. Although both snipe and ducks are moving constantly on windy days, especially when some of them have been disturbed by hunters, this circumstance is to the advantage of only the duck hunter, who waits at selected spots where the ducks may be expected to come down. The snipe hunter enjoys no such benefit from the movement of the birds, for he finds them scattered over a suitable feeding ground and he must approach near enough to them to secure shots whenever the birds rise. Often they are so much on edge that there are few chances of shooting at them within range.

Most hunters try to approach snipe against the wind, for while the birds will turn their courses momentarily into the wind, their final progress after straightening out is with the wind or at least diagonally towards the hunter. An approach with the wind, though making it likely that through scent or sound one of these birds will detect the hunter sooner, has the advantage of giving him possibly two or three seconds in which it will come a little closer to him and be at a lower level than when it has got away in its swift race down the wind. One must be extremely quick, however, to take advantage of the moment or so in which the bird is in position to afford a favorable shot.

Some experienced snipe shooters believe that the best approach to the birds is across the wind or, even better, so as to make less than a right angle with it. Since the birds rise against the wind, some of them are likely to afford good crossing shots.

The general drabness and appearance of inertia in the wet lands in winter and the explosive vitality and spasmodic speed of the snipe, full of untamed agility and energy, are not inconsistent. The snipe's manner of feeding is one in which interruption is particularly unwelcome to it. It must engage in an absorbing search for its food, concentrating its senses in an exploration of the mud to the greatest extent consistent with readiness for escape. It is not remarkable that it is a bundle of taut and springy alertness and quickness and that in the more or less forbidding marshes it finds the surest provision for its requirements.

Despite the comparative safety of the snipe in the marsh, seldom does it allow itself to be caught unaware in the hunting season and is off like a small catapult when danger is really near. Some idea of the tension of its existence and the extent of its immediate alarm must come from its rasping, incisive note. Aspiration is an objective quality of the voice, and, from the human side, one may wonder whether there is not also exasperation over the rude disturbance that has driven it away from its contented probing in the mire. Undoubtedly there is some deep equivalent of complaint, disgust, or resentment in the small frame that hurtles, veers, and rockets forward and upward in the tempo of its unmistakable notes, following each other at well-spaced intervals that serve to emphasize the directness of their incentive, whether it be agitation or a signal of danger to others.

The swift rising of the snipe on all sides when their grounds are invaded is at a level of interest and excitement for which there is no comparable experience in the marsh. Sometimes the nearest birds do not rise first, and many a surprised hunter when aiming or firing at a bird about to get out of range realizes that another has sprung into the air at a closer quarter.

The behavior of snipe is least excitable on quiet, warm days in winter. When they rise, they can start immediately in the direction of escape, having no wind with which to contend. Unless approached rather closely, they seem reluctant to leave their feeding, and their flight is lower and more direct than in windy weather. In this trend of their existence they give the hunter a consistent chance of matching his skill against their less bewildering dispersion and movements.

The marshy flats most attractive to snipe are not subject to true tide movement, but more or less brackish water may be forced over them with strong winds from the Gulf. In that case the birds leave them temporarily and become more plentiful wherever lands at the next measurably higher level are soft enough to attract them. Snipe shooting in its easiest form is open then to the hunter. The birds crowd to the low prairies, wild pasture lands, and old fields, even in well-settled farming neighborhoods or on the outskirts of towns. Pursuit of snipe on such surfaces is a much less laborious matter than going after them in the boggy lands to which they are confined ordinarily.

As though relying on a universal disposition to discourage the pursuit of game in the spring, prevented usually by law if not by common reason and consent, snipe lose much of their restlessness and wariness at that season. Often when flushed, they fly lazily, even steadily, and only for very short distances before dropping almost inertly to the cover again. Even their notes are less emphatic. Such birds are undoubtedly migrants returning from a winter spent in the tropics and are making a sojourn in the lush Louisiana marshes to fatten themselves before continuing on their way to far northern breeding grounds.

Usually when snipe are disturbed, they come down again at no great distance. There are times when they tower to considerable heights and come together in small wisps that perform bold, aerial evolutions, spanning the sky in a coursing, commanding flight that is one of the finest spectacles of the marsh scene in winter.

CHAPTER XIV

High Tide of Spring

IN THE FAR SOUTH much of April is at once a delightful and a baffling time in which to select outdoor objectives. Everywhere there are billows of vegetation and a drifting sweetness in the air; with them come endless shades of green and overflowing, overlapping bird music. The succulence of foliage and the vapory mildness of the air become almost a single medium for the diffusion of sunshine. Groves, farm lands, and rich swamps or other woodland swirl together in a flood of verdure, deep yet penetrable, that blots out all traces of bareness or sharpness. Birds move about with an ease and certitude as buoyant as the traveling of their calls and songs.

One of the most astonishing manifestations of bird life comes to the lowlands in this season of unmeasured luxuriance in all life. Swallows gather by thousands over moist, open ground, which is a continuous and variously yellow or white sheet of ragwort and fleabane in bloom. The air at a low level is filled with insects numerous beyond computation and furnishes the swallows with a feast seldom equalled. The birds skim, wheel, and float or bank at heights ranging from one or two to a hundred or more feet above the earth. A very great proportion of them are the green and white tree swallows, though at times there are many of the more colorful and graceful barn swallows. Sweeping in many directions, curving into and out of each other's paths, they form a bewildering pattern of animation and gleaming color. Some of them seem almost ready to rest on the flowers, coming down or going up a few wing beats, striving against a breeze or shearing off with it. This carnival of drifting and feasting goes on quietly, except for some twittering, and when it is at its height the climactic point in the spring exuberance has been reached. Marshy places, the vicinity of ponds, and the shores of lakes and lagoons are the most attractive places for the congregations of swallows. Occasionally a few of them come to rest on the tops of bushes or on the bending stems of sedges, stout grasses, or other low plants, contrasting singularly in their sedate appearance with the array of birds in the air.

The full-blown beauty and balminess of the coastal spring has another phase in woods of beech, magnolia, oak, hickory, and smaller trees that vary the pinewoods region, especially in the vicinity of small streams. At all times this growth has a pleasing and unmistakable delineation more striking than the merged luxuriance of swampy woods. The influence of spring at its peak gives it an almost intangible richness and delicacy, patent but indefinable. Some of it comes from the odors of woodland shrubs in bloom. Nearest the coast these woodlands have a crowded growth, with low-massing foliage and are retreats of the main body of forest-loving birds. Among the pine hills farther inland they fringe the streams and are most striking for the dark, sandy slopes beneath them and the great size of their white and basket oaks, tulip-trees, black and sweet gums, magnolias, and hickories.

Some of the rarer migratory birds, especially warblers, are most fully in their element in woods of the type just mentioned, the first of a somewhat upland character to be found on the way back from the coast. Like a purveyor of jewels, a particularly bright, fresh day after a late spring storm may fill the trees with intensely colored, curiously patterned kinds of birds, such as the Blackburnian, golden-winged, and even the very rare Bachman warbler; the more numerous but equally beautiful magnolia and black-throated green warblers; the gem-like parula, or blue yellow-back; the always engaging redstart; and the agile, volatile black-and-white warbler, which invests the woods with the thoroughness of an invading army, running up and down the trunks and limbs of the trees, darting cleanly from one spot to another, now an unmistakable figure, next an incarnation of woodland delicacy. Most of these birds have the same elusiveness and are almost as evanescent as the colors of the rainbow. The revelation of their identity is a spontaneous occurrence. One moment there is an indistinguishable wisp of feathers, the next it resolves itself into a presence as distinct as that of the cardinal or the blue jay, yet none of them ever seems commonplace.

After the departure of most of the transient warblers and other birds purely migratory at this latitude, the feeling of summer comes into the air. It does not exert its full force at once but merly cancels the possibility of any lingering chilliness in a kind of aftermath of spring that settles on the coastlands. It is often a spell of flawless weather and may last a fortnight or more. It is a distillation of the best in spring, summer, and even autumn. Verdure, temperature, light, and atmospheric balance are perfect in this peaceful reign. Spring gales of the coast are over, and the tornadoes feared farther inland during this crucial interlude are rare or unknown. This brief time of serene-tempered weather may include the first ten or twelve days of May. It brings full blooming of the magnolia, ripening of mulberries, culmination of spring fishing, general nesting of birds, and final, sometimes most fascinating, phases of migration on a limited scale.

Man and the rest of animate creation surrender quickly to the pleasant influences of these lingering days of spring. Their blandness spreads even over the Gulf, where the sea birds, waiting for the end of vernal disturbances, begin to collect on shell reefs and low, sandy or muddy islands to lay their eggs on bare sand and shells or in rudely formed nests. In or near woodlands this is the season to catch repeated glimpses of yellow-billed cuckoos, slipping swiftly, often silently, across spaces among fresh-foliaged crowns of tall trees, to hear the constant melody of the wood thrush, the accented whistling of red-eyed vireos, and the rich, flush notes of orchard orioles as they occupy every leafy background in town and country.

On the sandy, wooded coast of Mississippi there is an ethereal mildness when the quiet ripple from the beach and the scarcely audible rustle in high-standing, open-armed oaks, pines, and hickories drift together in a low voice of conciliation and fulfillment. A reflection of these sounds comes from the lisping, indolent, forest-born trill of the parula warbler, low but vibrantly distinct and in harmony with the quiet sounds of the woods and the seaside. Other bird notes—clear, as those of the titmouse, or shrill, like the call of the crested flycatcher, or, again, very gentle, as the pensive intonation of the wood pewee—have their places in these surroundings, but none embodies them as effectually as those of the parula.

For brightness and luxuriance of vegetation as summer approaches, there is nothing quite equal to lands that border the Mississippi. Starting with willows at the water's edge and sweeping across the gentle double slopes of the levee, an unbroken fabric of light green, puckered into thickets and groves, spreads over deeply fertile fields to fade away in an uncertain horizon. It trembles and glistens in the prismatic sunlight of these days when both spring and summer are in the air. Seen from the crown of the levee in the fading afternoon light, it has a peculiar radiance that transforms a country of no remarkable beauty except the massing of its greenery.

Birds that appear in these expanses are lively and abundant. Red-winged blackbirds call tunefully from willow tops or chatter sharply as they launch restlessly into short, wavering flights. Orchard orioles cling to swinging sprays or, pausing in tremulous flight, sing unchecked in mid-air. The surprisingly beautiful painted bunting, with a modest but pleasing song that gathers up the freshness of the fields, moves in short stages where there are low, scattered trees, delivering its fixed yet never tiresome bit of music at each stop. The last week in April is the time, if ever, to get glimpses of the bobolink in its spring dress and hear catches of its song in these cultivated lands along the Mississippi. A few may make short visits to patches of oats and rich pasture lands. At this season, the bobolink is distinctive in appearance and habits, in contrast to the greater numbers that come in fall to the rice fields and wild lands, and, having changed plumage, merge more or less with the crowding flocks of red-winged blackbirds.

When the bird life proper to the coast country in the summer months has settled down for the season, it is paradoxical to find migratory stragglers of other species still about on their way north. Among small birds, Wilson's thrush and cedar waxwing have been known to remain as late as the beginning of June, and several others, notably the bay-breasted warbler, linger to the very end of days that retain some springlike character, a period that goes at least to the middle of May. Much of the summering bird population has brought out broods by this time, yet in the same pecan, live oak, or fruit trees with nesting mockingbirds, orchard orioles, and other distinctly southern species may be bay-breasted warblers, which are uncommon even at the peak of their migration. They seem actually more identified with this environment and less restless than when observed earlier. Some that I saw one year on May 16 in the grounds of a home in the sugar plantation district west of New Orleans behaved with so much familiarity that at first I could scarcely credit their presence. The weather was settled, and they appeared as much established as the atmospheric conditions. Audubon has recorded, in fact, that he took specimens in the middle of summer in a cotton field in West Feliciana parish, Louisiana. While those that he saw may have been birds in an early return from the north, as happens with some other species, it is more likely that they were individuals that did not reach their far northern breeding grounds but loitered unmated in a climate not congenial to their nesting habits.

CHAPTER XV

Bird Dwellers of a Sugar Plantation

SUGAR PLANTATIONS of southern Louisiana lack today a good deal of the physical background that distinguished them several decades ago. They are still pleasant environments and distinctive retreats for birds, but hardly in the same way as formerly when even the most improved properties along the Mississippi River were in a setting where nature had been disturbed only slightly. Outlines of an unobtrusive levee, a live oak grove that sheltered the home, fields in cultivation, cleared land in disuse, and the swampy woodland back from the river blended in summer into a smooth, tranquilizing scene. The peace and abundance of the country were in visible possession. Improvements and cultivation, instead of dominating the outlook, sank into it as a token of truce between man and nature. Even though the needs of civilized living were there, the wilderness was always within touch.

However it may impress its human dwellers, a sugar plantation of the type that existed chiefly at the turn of the century is a never failing asylum of birds. A balance between new cultivation and long-standing growths becomes a leafy vesture exuding color and freshness and contributing to the prosperity of its feathered frequenters. On the surface, its whole purpose seems to be to provide a lively bivouac of abounding and musical birds. There are orchard orioles, mockingbirds, painted buntings, crested flycatchers, cuckoos, red-winged blackbirds, meadow larks, mourning doves, and a dozen others immediately within sight or sound as one comes into the bland, relaxing midst of a sugar plantation at its best.

Against the reassuring assemblage of familiar figures living as unchallenged tenants of garden and grove is the contingent of birds immemorially present in the wilder lands back from the course of the river, indigenous inhabitants of the swamps that once made up this entire region. Out of range of even the sounds of the plantation, they have their chief haunts along old drainage canals overarched with luxuriant summer growths, in coves of tupelo, maple, and ash, and back in the somber corridors of cypresses. A ramble in these and other places that make an uncertain border about a sugar plantation brings to light such birds in an unpredictable sequence. The note of the shy hooded warbler resounds from the swampy tangle, and ventriloqual calls of the yellow-breasted chat come from thickets of willows. A purple gallinule may be flushed from its cover at the edge of a canal to run and splash quickly but awkwardly into new hiding, a precaution, if danger were really present, that should be taken as hastily as possible by a mark as shining as this hyacinthine, yellow-legged inhabitant of marshy retreats.

Farther into the swampy forest are places where wood ducks whir with strange, murmuring undertones between the crowns of the cypresses. In the morning or late afternoon, a view of rare white ibises above the tops of the trees will show them flying abreast in a wavering line and flapping and sailing their way between distant points that belong in the economy of their lives. A pileated woodpecker, aloof in the fastness of the swamp, shatters the prevailing silence with high-pitched notes, which seem to come from everywhere at once. A chance sight of the bird would reveal it in high, bold flight among the taller trees.

Far-reaching sugar-cane fields have only an incidental bird life; their luxuriant color and appearance of freshness are without corresponding attraction for most species of birds. In the heat and sharp brightness of midsummer they offer little shelter and scarcely any food for winged tenants. The corn, pea, and hay fields that flank them are more suitable for a few of the summer birds. The indigo bunting, sharply brilliant in the sun, sings from the top of a cornstalk or its perch on a dead tree left standing in a field. Less exposed, the painted bunting frees its light, sweet, quickly delivered song. Wandering orchard orioles move indecisively in the thatch of the corn, and from the nearest brush or thicket comes the exact phrasing of the towhee. Somewhere among the pea vines a grasshopper sparrow utters its quaint, feeble notes. The silent little rough-winged swallows circle above the shimmering surfaces with something less than their usual adroitness. A hint of listlessness steals into the notes and movements of most birds. At least the yellow-breasted chat, concealed in a border of elders and willows, sings with its usual vigor in the drenching sunshine of morning and late afternoon. "Whoort, whoort, whoort" or, as a southern farmer transcribed it to me, "hot, hot, hot," is the main theme of its song, which it bends to many variations and accents.

The invariably entertaining summer bird life of the plantation environs is that of the live oaks, pecans, or other trees about the home. The birds' day starts shortly before dawn, usually with the rounded whistling of the purple martin. Mockingbirds, singing at night when there is moonlight, have no regular schedule. Cardinals may sing off and on before day even without moonlight. Orchard orioles are the most consistent of the true songsters of the morning. They begin their performances at or a little before dawn. The cooing of the dove, the prolonged, gently whistling note of the wood pewee, and the shrill call of the crested flycatcher are accompanying notes in the growing light.

The attachment of birds to the groves of the older plantations is a very natural one. In them they have ample food and shelter and greater safety from wild enemies than elsewhere. Those that are not migratory remain in the vicinity throughout the year and occupy the same nesting sites from spring to spring, while migrants become established in the habit of returning to a well-tried summer home.

Besides its dwelling grounds, a sugar plantation on the Mississippi has sometimes another marked attraction for birds. Outside the levee may lie a wide "batture," or kind of foreshore, built up by deposits of silt in high stages of the stream and uncovered by the falling of the water level at other times. In the course of a few seasons of moderate levels a considerable little forest develops or flourishes on these chance lands. It consists of fast-growing trees of the lowland soil—sycamore, hackberry, honey locust, willow, swamp privet, cottonwood, deciduous holly, or winterberry, swamp haw and dogwood, and even a few larger trees, but never live oaks, which are unable to stand even brief submergence during their early growth. On the other hand, the soil is too dry during most of the year to encourage the cypress.

The slight, deciduous forest on the "batture" is a reservoir of surplus bird supply for the surrounding fields and trees. Its quiet shelter makes it a mecca for some of the shy migrants that begin to straggle southward in middle or late summer. The little known Philadelphia vireo, golden-winged warbler, worm-eating warbler, and other less common species, as well as many redstarts and black-and-white warblers, descend on these places in sudden and numerous arrays. It is a special little bird drama, a side scene in the general manifestation of summer bird life.

The bower-like character of the casual and limited woodlands, shading the clean, gray sand of the riverbank, is unlike any other aspect in this part of the world and provides a retreat somewhat like that from which the bird visitors have come. Overlooking the surface of the river not far below it and isolated from the flat fields behind the levee, it is an illusion of upland country. It is easy to observe birds here. The rising river may come over these variable banks in spring or early summer, but when the river is down, a "batture" is the best drained place in southern Louisiana. Sometimes these strange woods are of exceptional regularity and beauty, luxuriant but not tangled, and with a smooth floor, evenly spaced trees, pleasant glades, and shady or sunny vistas, through which the birds are more readily visible than in the swamps or high trees. Matching the suggestion of high inland woods in these places is the broad surface of the river, as placid as a mountain lake and reflecting the blue of the sky and the great white clouds of summer. Only the humid heat makes it certain that the scene is still one in the lowlands.

In its own way, winter bird life on the plantation is as animated as that of summer. What it lacks in music it makes up in energy and freedom of movement. It is full of constant shifts and regroupings. One day the center of activity is the borders of fields and exposed thickets, the next, closer shelter of oak groves or patches of small, half-leafy trees. Sociability controls most of the winter birds, and, except in the worst weather, they have a way of displaying themselves as though on a holiday excursion. Although they come together in loose companies in which there are constant minor changes, it is never as easy at any other time to recognize the clear identity of as many species of birds appearing side by side. The continual fighting, chasing, and skulking among summer birds are not characteristic of these winter assemblages. Consistent but less restless activity and a bolder energy take their place.

The cheeriness of these winter groups comes out especially in white-throated sparrows, whisking confidently in short flights or pausing long enough in fence corners, shrubbery, and briar patches under the ample spread of live oaks to set up a fragment of the music that distinguishes them in their northern nesting grounds. Usually in the same places with them, but far less numerous, are house wrens, dodging in and out of whatever cover they can find, and the still rarer, smaller, and more furtive winter wrens. Cardinal, tufted titmouse, and Carolina wren are native figures that join this bustling crowd. More in the open and keeping somewhat to itself, trim, erect, and inclined to sedateness in color and manner, the phoebe bird sits on shriveled stalk, bare twig, or other convenient perch. If a keen wind is astir, it faces it without apparent discomposure and, except for a few feathers on the flanks, keeps its plumage intact. In more sheltered spots, a characteristic sight is a small, flurrying crowd of chickadees, kinglets, palm and myrtle warblers, sometimes the blue-headed vireo and the pine warbler, even a gnatcatcher, braving winter days in the lowlands.

The residue of vegetation in the plantation fields in winter makes them very attractive to ground-loving birds, which find not only a harvest of grass and weed seeds but many hibernating insects. Killdeers, pipits, meadow larks, and savanna sparrows have no better places to feed. Near the borders of the woods, robins, bluebirds, and goldfinches are among the more conspicuous members of the winter throng. The swamp sparrow finds a congenial cover in weedy ditches or in the lower growths about the remote edges of fields.

Throngs of blackbirds, the most striking displays of bird life on the plantation in winter, are scattered often on bare or grassy ground or in the trees. Sometimes there are clouds of grackles, red-wings, cowbirds, and rusty blackbirds. Their restless movements and confused chattering and whistling are amazing. They are most on the go in gray, chilly weather after wind and rain. On bright, settled days their travels are principally in the early mornings and late afternoons. Variably loose or compact flocks on their way between different feeding grounds or between feeding and roosting places, may stretch out across the country for a mile or more.

CHAPTER XVI

Glimpses and Impressions of the Mississippi Coast

Back of the Beach—Morning Phantasy—Assault on
Summer—Hurricane Weather

THE PLEASANT SCENES of the shore leave so little to be
desired that dwellers or visitors on the Mississippi
coast are inclined to postpone an exploration of what
lies behind it. Resilient lines of the beach and ever-
present interplay of lights and motions fix a spell that
is not broken willingly. Chance or necessity are most
likely to lead its contented captives away from it to
recessed reaches of woods and inland waters.

Not many steps away from the beach, the essence of
the bright, seaside woodland prevails over the flurry
and flutter of the outer spaces. The quiet rustle of high
pinetops is a touch from the sea, but a calm, sylvan
stability is stamped in the forms of fine forest trees
that rise uncrowded and as a loose canopy from a floor
perpetually brown with fallen pine needles. The air
among oaks, hickories, and pines is undisturbed and

full of the fresh, compounded scents of mint, bay, and resinous leaves and branches. To go from the jostling sea winds to the steadying balm within these first woods is one of the rich wonders of the coast country. Such grounds where, in the past, deer and wild turkeys lived confidently, must have been favorite haunts of the Indian aborigines. The primeval quiet, if not all the wild creatures, is still part of them.

The concentration of many of the beauties of the coast country is greatest in the upper, winding reaches of Biloxi Bay. The sea is here only in the coming and going of its tides. Deep or shallow, the waters are placid, wedging variously into the wooded plateau. Whether they are streamlike or lakelike and even marshy, they match the backgrounds of low bluffs, piney levels, and the more darkly wooded hollows. The mouth of a small, wandering river, coming out of the low, rounded pine hills, is the focus of their perspective. Here is the end or the beginning of acquaintance with what lies towards the sea or back among the silences of the uplands.

The first hour of light over the summer beach or back in wooded grounds of coast cottages repays at least one early rising a season. There are more unusual sensations crowded into this time than into the rest of the day. It is wonderful merely to look out over the brimming smoothness of the incoming tide, like a great trough of dark mercury swung within the visible arc of the horizon, pulsing hardly perceptibly against the sands or breakwaters of the shores. An infinity of perceptions comes from the tangy, vapory air, full of the loosened scent of the sea. It translates the rolling of the tide, the capricious wafting of light winds.

Signs of light and life ready to emerge from the dusk and immobility spread slowly. The flat splash of a leaping mullet leaves a silvery cascade that sparkles momentarily over darker water. Little plovers or other beach birds call with a subdued melody as they move in curving flight from point to point along the shore. Pelicans labor almost ominously in long-enduring flight that rises and falls near the level of the horizon.

Before the whole world is awake, changeless distinctions that make up the quality of this unfailingly beautiful coast are unmistakable, yet tinged with unreality. In the faint, even light, silhouetted pines, wind-pressed live oaks, little coves and marshes, mixed distances of points and woody backgrounds are yielding but definite to sight. Objects furnish but do not crowd the reaches of space. There are neither great light nor great shadows, only an easy clearness in all outlines, a freedom of view without abruptness or emptiness. Something of the unsubstantiality of a bubble or the fluidity of water and clouds comes from the pallor and diffusion of morning light. It is a picture perfected and motionless, a fragile, almost glassy creation that awaits the disturbance of motions, sounds, and the rising light and animation of the day.

Quiet and stillness envelop beach, water, sheltering oaks, dusky ravines, yards, open spaces of pinewoods. Whatever moves does so as if in another world. Early fishermen go about silently. A night-prowling racoon or opossum slips off from garden or back fence to the shelter of undergrowth. The home with open door, an empty hammock under the trees, fishing tackle on the porch, a mockingbird balancing with lifted wings at the edge of the walk belong with the haunting intangibles of a picture of fixed objects and unburdened spaces of the seaside before the coming of broad daylight.

Heat of late August in the sandy, pine-wooded region of the coast brings on sometimes a dramatic turn in the procession of the seasons. Before a change, the dog days drag on under a deluge of sunshine, smooth waters of the sound glitter, a shiny stillness envelops the pines, and a golden glare settles on the beach. The whole world seems focused in a concentration of static brilliance, of metallic inertness, relieved only by drifting gulls and terns, dragonflies that hover in the air, or a tiny yellow warbler moving deftly, like a glint of fervid light, among the oaks and cedars.

On an afternoon in these breathless and shimmering days the heat reaches a new intensity. Suddenly there is a mutter from the north, the faintest stir in the air. The burning blue above the pines begins to fade. Against it there is a different and barely perceptible glimmer of quivering light. Presently a slashing streak of lightning cuts across the sky over the treetops. The thunder cloud grows higher, crooked webs of lightning become more frequent, the rumbling is more menacing.

As though recoiling before threatened impact of oncoming forces sweeping the pinetops, the air is electric, seems to grow thinner and clearer, objects are magnified and are sharply defined, a sense of nascent life and motion spreads over all. In these moments of suspense fall the first loose, spattering raindrops, and a light trembling comes to the pine boughs. The stir grows in reviving puffs of air, and finally come racing wind, tangled lightning, reverberating thunder, and drenching rain that drives beachward and seaward. The last fierce struggle of summer has been ended by the salutary might of the gathering forces of the inlands.

Another day breaks with new sparkle in the air, kept alive in the forenoon by a light offshore wind. Open pinewoods, boggy thickets, and bushy clearings teem with newly arrived migrant birds—little flycatchers, warblers, tanagers—some of them present for the first time since they went northward in spring. Thus the potence and charm of nature return irresistibly after the trying days of a summer mood. The heat may return for a time, abundant signs of summer remain, crisp winds and energy of bird migration will give way uncertainly to indolent, vagrant breezes and listless movements among the feathered tenants of pinewoods and gum sloughs. Days will not be quite the same again, however, summer in its full panoply cannot be expected back for another cycle of the year. It is a momentous change to have all started with a blue-black thunder squall, rising like a genie over the hot, pine-clad stretches behind the coast.

More than any other kind of weather that plays over it, a late summer or autumnal gale, especially one of tropical hurricane intensity, changes greatly the appearance of the coast. The one thing above all else that distinguishes this part of the world under most conditions is its blandness and reassuring distinctness as a lodgment by the sea. Though fierce winds and deluges of rain cannot wreck its essential integrity as mainland, they leave nothing of the intangible qualities that mark it in fair weather. Outlines, colors, and every scenic component fades out in the gray mastery of the tempest and the heaving waters cascading high against the shore.

The hours or days that precede the hurricane are more subtle than either the prevailing temper of the coast scene or its eclipse in the height of the storm. Wan tints come and go in the uncertainly speeding clouds; a lurid light falls on the water; pines grow pale and unsubstantial in a palsied sunshine or regain full stature and inky sharpness in momentary shadows from the darker scud. Everywhere is something that suggests dissolution or collapse of familiar scenes. Even the air seems ready to draw together, to be distended, by turns, to be moving in centrifugal impulses or nearing a goal that wavers beyond it. The sense of swaying and shifting, of alternation between vacuum and pressure, replaces the ordinary blowing of the wind, and all the sure fabric of things is in seeming readiness to pass away or fall in ruin with it.

At its height, the gray avalanche of waves and rain batters perilously at everything that it can reach. With renewed bursts of force, it dwarfs reliance on the steadfastness of the shore, so that even the substance of things out of its reach is lost in an aqueous envelopment. The blur of landmarks emerges in a shifting of the wind and the rain, only to vanish in the returning pall. The only certainty is the absence of any appearance that has seemed unchangeable. It is not until the rain has ended and the wind has slackened that the beach, in spite of colorless sky and high, tumbling waves, recovers some of its distinctive character.

CHAPTER XVII

Three Seasons in One

LACKING ONLY the assurance of full leafage and untrammeled dispersion and music of birds, spring or an equivalent steps right into the midst of the lowland scene many times when it should be winter. It is strange to see mostly brown fields and bare woods bathed in a persuasive imitation of the radiance and many of the colors associated with genial, expansive days of another season. A warm gloss of russet, dull gold, and bronze brightens in the sunlight, and narrow traceries of green revive and broaden under the same urgent encouragement. Hard, weathered outlines cannot survive the light flood of luminance and vapory mellowness that descends on marsh, swamp, and ragged thickets. The confluence of forms and colors restores the smoothness of the coast country. A wash of sunshine overlies it all, tinting impartially live oaks, edges of fields, drab forms of leafless trees, and the waters of the marsh. The pale, yielding blue of the sky, fringed and patched with white, barely drifting clouds, seems never more closely welded with the earth. Altogether, it is the return of a repeatedly familiar picture erased now and then by sharp, sudden thrusts of cold, hardly the disclosure of something different, as in the changing advance of spring.

As inextricable parts of winter at the latitude of the Gulf Coast and especially as it appears in the lowlands, days like spring or Indian summer are more consistently recurrent than any other manifestation of the weather in the span of this southern season. The sequences, however, are unpredictable. A week past it might have seemed that nothing would stop a strong vernal tide, a few days ago there was a wintry rain, and today the quiet and mellowness of late fall cover the contradictory accomplishments of frost and warm winds. Backward, forward, and part of the way side by side, the three seasons follow a labyrinthine course from the first moderately cold day in November to the last one in February, after which there is a light green mantle in many directions; if it is not spring every day, it will be the next or the day after that, in spite of any disagreement by the thermometer.

In its effect on native plant life, spring actually starts in this strange land before autumn is gone. The tassel-like bloom of the cypress hangs in plain sight on the bare trees even before Christmas, and the flower-leaves of the maple, brilliantly crimson or rosy saffron against the grayness of the swamps, appear at least by the beginning of the year. If only to a slight extent, that is a start for spring. So is the occasional singing of the cardinal at this time. It has been autumn by the calendar so recently that leaves are falling still from some of the trees, giving a rather direct retrospect of a season supposedly left behind. Some evergreen trees, shrubs, or vines, especially live oak, wax myrtle, yaupon, and smilax, are distinctive in any of the seasonal aspects of which they are a part.

Thus by a series of relays, leaps, and meteorological somersaults, a rather trying period in the far southern year carries out the functions of annual renewals without remaining too long in any fixed position. Memories of a few days of icy blasts in this damp region, however, are sufficient to make the period in which they are possible a time of menace to those who have been trustful. Expectation of mid-winter days continuously springlike is perpetual, many times justified, but likely to encourage a false confidence in the possibility of escape from any but the most considerate visits of winter. It is usually when such optimism is greatest that the rebuff is most staggering. From such experiences the lowlander should learn that during something less than four months all thought of evading real winter weather should be entirely negative or at least noncommittal; he should be immune to surprise, and by no means center too great hope on what may seem a time of nature's unreserved generosity. With such reinforcements of prudence and the constant respites of sunshine and quieted winds, the passage of the colder part of the year will be judged more discerningly for its occasional lapses from the general leniency of the weather in these parts.

I have always thought of the coast winter as being divided into the part before Christmas and that afterward. Moderately cold weather is sometimes more constant in the first part than in the second, although the reversals of mildness are most overwhelming in the latter. There is always the possibility, though a slight one, of a year when there is no temperature as low as freezing after the middle of January, so that by early March spring is an old season. Not unusually a good many mild days come in January. On the other hand, the lowest temperature ever known at the coast, recorded as zero or a few degrees above, according to localities, was on February 13 one year, and the deepest snow, nearly nine inches, fell on February 14 a few years earlier. The latter part of February, however, belongs chiefly or entirely to spring.

Under the more serious punishment of winter, the lowlands seem exceptionally desolate after some of the balmy days. There is a complete about-face, not only in the temperature but in all atmospheric conditions. The landscape adds to the deception. The dullness of groves and swamps whipped by north winds, the pale coloring of water and fields, and the haphazard, meaningless greenery that has survived or defies frost preserves no summery recollections as rain, sleet, cutting blasts, and impenetrable clouds overwhelm the evanescent land. The scene lacks the crispness and endurance that stand out on cold days in the uplands and merely wilts under the heavy engagement of winter forces. In its contrast to many milder days, real winter weather comes always as something alien in this land. All the native tints and textures disappear. Things that give expression to the landscape on balmy days are no medium for conveying the beauty of the winter.

The contradictions in the lowland winter come to light in the incessant fluctuations of bird life. Comparatively few of the smaller birds that nest in this region remain through the winter. A good many of the water birds conspicuous in summer are gone also. Lively, hardy strangers from more northern latitudes come to replace them. If it were not for the ever-familiar cardinal, red-wing, grackle, Carolina wren, tree swallow, and a scant dozen others familiar throughout the lowlands at most times, the cast of the bird assemblage would be altered completely. There is no dearth of the visiting bird life almost anywhere during the whole winter season, and much of it arrives considerably before the nominal beginning of the period and remains somewhat after it has ended in the full opening of spring. In bright weather, birds are conspicuous in swamps, drier woods, and open places, often as lively as the display of summer birds. When they need shelter, there is seldom lack of it.

The promiscuous feathered crowds, roaming from cover to cover, changing feeding grounds, becoming scarce or numerous with varying fortunes of the weather, stir the soberer precincts of the land chosen for this free adventure and exploration. The hermit thrush has its confident sojourn in underbrush of moist woodland where the hooded warbler was at home in summer; the yellow-bellied sapsucker, bringing a new touch of manners and colors, clings to the trunk of ash or maple that a while back was the shady abode of the Acadian flycatcher. White-throated sparrows, house wrens, palm and myrtle warblers, moving with casual sprightliness among the thickets, make a mixed company with cardinals, titmice, or other true natives of the swamplands. Little birds of short flight that spend most of their time moving lightly and quickly on the ground rise in small flurries when they are disturbed in field or pasture. Probably all but one in many thousands of them are savanna sparrows, and the exception is the rare Leconte's sparrow, rare, at least, in this region. Their constant presence and abundance are convincing evidence of the attraction for winter bird life. Preferring moister, more protected places than the others, swamp sparrows cheep and call variously in weed-choked ditches. In the last light of a misty, chilly winter evening, their voices rise in a hesitant, conflicting chorus that breaks oddly over the colorless solitude of the flat lands on the verge of darkness. The sight and the sounds are among unmistakable distinctions of the lowlands in winter.

Birds that come towards the end of winter, when persistence of snow blankets, the freezing of the ground or dwindling of food supplies on trees and bushes have made more northern localities uninhabitable, are the boldest and most restless and tumultuous of the throng of winter visitors. They rove in shifting confusion over town and countryside, seeking out new harvests of seeds, berries, leaf-buds, and inactive or hibernating insects. Some find themselves prosperously adrift in the approaching spring and, with the certainty of plenty all about them, loiter on while the tide of travel for some winter birds is beginning to turn northward. Cedar waxwings, fresh contingents of robins, northern-bred individuals of the red-wing and other blackbirds, and, in severe winter spells, the purple finch are the most important of these late winter arrivals. Robins and waxwings are especially prominent and active in their wanderings and concentrations. The greatest numbers appear sometimes on springlike days after a cold spell, leading to an impression that their arrival coincides with an early advent of spring and that they have come from farther south instead of having preceded a southward extension of the cold. Several weeks of intermittent visitations of icy weather may lie ahead in more northern localities, and the birds remain where they can build up their reserves of fat and energy before venturing a return. When most of them have gone, spring is very much on its way.

CHAPTER XVIII

Nondescript Habitats of Birds

AN OBSERVER accustomed to a familiar display of certain species of birds in most countrysides has the surprising experience of finding many of them either unusual or missing in lowland localities in Louisiana that might seem suited to them. They are the kinds that in other districts overflow into the clearings from surrounding woods but that have never had well-established habitats anywhere in the lowlands. In agricultural areas of the coastal region there are only uncertain colonies of species indigenous to ordinarily well-drained surfaces. Not only do drainage and cultivation in the lowlands fail to attract some of the birds numerous in a country of somewhat upland character but they limit the presence of most swamp-loving species, so that, as a whole, bird life in the more accessible parts of the lowlands has a rather changeable and indefinable character.

In the region commonly above tidewater in lowland Louisiana there are only five primitive habitats of birds: deep fresh-water marshes; wet, but not usually submerged, savannas or prairies; live oak ridges; cypress and tupelo swamps; and moist or wet but rarely flooded hardwood forest growths. In southwestern Louisiana there is a well-elevated prairie district. The integrity, or distinctness, of these types of surface has become obscure in many areas as the result of drainage and cultivation. Such mixture of surfaces and growths leads to a very irregular distribution of much of the bird life. The chance trees or bushes about the edges of fields or on abandoned lands have no special attraction for any particular species of bird. Native kinds find temporary shelter or nesting places among them, migrants or wanderers linger about them in the days of their sojourn in the lowlands. Species that would be found ordinarily in distinctive surroundings in other parts of the country mingle in a haphazard way on farming or plantation lands.

There are so few birds definitely characteristic of the peculiarly drained lands that the heterogeneous nature of the bird life is really more striking than any display of consistency with which some birds spread over the open or partly cleared spaces. The cultivated lands draw mostly the species that would never be in the region if all the swamps remained. So in spring or summer, at least, an unchanging group of swamp dwellers is in proximity to the various birds that inhabit only agricultural spaces or other drained land, causing an interesting and somewhat unpredictable variety.

Some of the unusual degrees of abundance or scarcity of birds generally considered as familiar species are very striking. Redheaded woodpeckers and bluebirds are absent from many localities for long periods and are more or less sporadic at all times. Except locally, especially about oak groves, the blue jay is rather irregular and uncommon. The chipping sparrow is an unknown species in the wet lands, and the chuck-will's-widow and whippoorwill are practically unheard or unseen at any time. Since there are no pines in the lowest coast country of Louisiana except its eastern extremity, nuthatches are lacking in its avifauna. The coastlands are deficient in spring in the presence of some of the small, exclusively migratory species normally dispersed in other types of country during the vernal migration, though in fall the case is entirely different and some species find the lowlands especially congenial—good places to loiter in their slow southward progress. This applies to two or three species of flycatchers, a number of kinds of warblers, scarlet tanager, and rose-breasted grosbeak.

Crested flycatchers, tufted titmice, kinglets, chiefly the ruby-crowned, robins, red-eyed vireos, summer tanagers, and white-throated sparrows are a group of species about as common in the less swampy woods and adjoining farm lands as in a different type of country.

Carolina wrens, grackles, and cardinals are present wherever there are trees, shrubs, and vines. Mockingbirds, of course, are inevitable followers of settlement and cultivation on a greater or less scale. Redwinged blackbirds, primarily inhabitants of the marsh, need only the encouragement of ponds, deep ditches, or boggy places to go anywhere else. The red-bellied woodpecker, though far less common, has an almost equally wide dispersion wherever there are trees. The pileated woodpecker, ordinarily a swamp-dwelling species, strays rather rarely to groves or single trees near the outskirts of its haunts, especially in the more remote localities. The fondness of the warbling vireo for shade trees is exemplified as well in the lowlands as elsewhere. Elms, willows, water oaks, and pecans, in groves, along streets or roads, and in yards, pastures, and orchids, are its favorite retreats.

The numbers of myrtle warblers vary greatly from winter to winter, but their dispersion is always general. From neighboring pinewoods or possibly more distant ones, a few pine warblers reach the lowlands in winter, preferring low groves or small thickets; it is unusual to find more than three or four in a day, and the most likely time for seeing them is early spring, at which season they become more scattered. There are many grounds near both swamps and farms that are suitable in summer for the yellow-breasted chat.

A group consisting of Acadian flycatchers, white-eyed vireos, and prothonotary, hooded, and Kentucky warblers is the most distinctive example of nonaquatic bird life in these lowlands. Though the parula warbler is not confined to these areas in the nesting season, it is seldom as common in other habitats as here.

About the only very distinct peculiarity of the bird life of lowland agricultural spaces is that in winter pipits and savanna sparrows are plentiful in fields and that in summer the painted bunting is a well-distributed species, orchard oriole especially abundant, yellow-billed cuckoo somewhat more plentiful than in other sections, and the prothonotary warbler rather likely to appear about the edges of fields bordering swampy places.

The extent of blending in the character of lowland bird aspects is especially striking in early spring. Restlessness among birds permanently present in these areas and others that are only migratory reaches an unusual level. The flexibility in the occurrence of a few species at this season is very stimulating to the interest of an observer. On a fresh, blustery day in mid-March there are most likely to be various birds that have no very regular occurrence in the reclaimed lowlands. Then, there is one that has been abundant during the winter but that has spent a great deal of its time in the swampier woods. This is the rusty blackbird, a small winter visitor from high latitudes. The males are glossy black, with a slight iridescence and flecks of bright tan, the females and probably most of the younger males slaty gray and several shades of brown. They make a somewhat paradoxical addition to easily observed bird life in this far southern section, mingling familiarly with cowbirds, grackles, and red-winged blackbirds about low thickets, fields, and pastures becoming green. They scatter on the spring air a jangling medley of creaking, whistling notes. The singing stops if they become alarmed and is followed by a few weak, flat chucks, which increase in number if the flock takes flight. The discordant and rather feeble music, not without a pleasant quality appropriate to the mildness of the season, presages return and reaccommodation of these travelers to the remote places of their origin. In these days they are as indigenous to the lowland scene as the redwing and the grackle.

Birds from much nearer breeding grounds than those of the rusty blackbird rank higher as surprising visitors in this region. The small, light-colored field sparrow, the finding of a dozen of which in a season would make them seem common, is one of such comparative rarities. A sedgy field or well-drained, bushy place is the most likely retreat for it. The vesper sparrow, frequenter of little disturbed pastures, is equally uncommon. Although there are briar patches, bushy ground, and other places that seem entirely suited to the song sparrow, it is one of the last birds to be expected in the lowland areas; thus one of the commonest birds of the northern countryside is almost a curiosity in most of southern Louisiana.

The swampy woods are less distinctive habitats in fall and winter than in the warmer parts of the year. They are tenanted by about the same species as the cultivated or partly cleared country, though they attract more individuals of species that seek shelter. The weather may bring about considerable changes from day to day, but, ordinarily, flickers, yellow-bellied sapsuckers, phoebes, house wrens, thrashers, robins, ruby-crowned kinglets, myrtle warblers, goldfinches, and white-throated sparrows show no particular discrimination but linger wherever the feeding is good. Tufted titmouse, Carolina wren, and cardinal, resident birds that have no great partiality to the swamps as nesting places, are about as widely dispersed in the colder months.

To see about all the birds it is possible to find in a day in the wooded or cultivated lowlands requires a considerable excursion. As noted already, there are some species having no widespread haunts in these lands but appearing by chance in various spots. Possibly one or two but hardly more of each of such kinds will be seen in a day's walk. On a day in early or middle April one may pass many thickets of willows beside ditches or ponds without finding a yellow warbler, yet if the exploration continues long enough, the attractive little singer will come to light. At the same season, the yellow-throated vireo, uttering its strange, guttural call from the top of cypress or oak, is a bird to be expected but not counted on. A slough in the damp woods is the most likely place to find a water-thrush, usually the species known as the northern water-thrush, sounding its quick, light note as it slips from sight after posturing briefly on low branch or rotting log.

Wood pewees, though by no means rare in the lowlands, may be strangely missing from most of the swampy or other woodland through which one passes. On the other hand, it is surprising to see even a single least flycatcher, which may make its appearance at the edge of a copse of low trees in the open. Towhees may be at only one or two shrubby thickets on the route traversed, and catbirds in sight only along a bushy ditch-side or in a shady patch of low trees. Tennessee warblers, traced by their faintly twittering songs, make a sunny clearing a notable point in the course of the day.

Abandoned farm lands in regions higher than the Louisiana coast district return in time to the character of surrounding woods or brush land, but in the swampy country land once drained and not subject through any cause to resubmergence never becomes like the original wooded swamps. If it goes back to woodland, the trees are principally oak, hackberry, sweet gum, sycamore, elm, and persimmon. If there have been cultivated pecans in such an area, volunteer growths of that species are likely to appear. The cypress and tupelo of the swamp have no place in these groups of trees, and ash, maple, and one or two other species making up much of the swamp growth represent a very small part of the regrowth on drained lands. There is no uniformity, of course, in these secondary woods, and most bird life has a random relationship to them. Almost any species not limited to very sharply defined habitats may come to them. All the birds occurring regularly in the lowlands, along with stragglers from other kinds of country, may resort to them. From season to season, practically any species except the swamp-loving warblers and, in migration, even occasional individuals of these, are of possible or likely occurrence, but it may take a long round to find some of them.

Besides the peculiarities of bird life due to the essential differences of the lowland district there are those that go with its geographical position. Like other parts of the Gulf Coast region, the Louisiana coastal strip is too far south to be the regular summer home of the catbird, robin, yellow warbler, Baltimore oriole, and field sparrow, which nest rather commonly in more northern parts of the Gulf States. Neither is this region, which is an almost subtropical part of the southern life zone, far enough north to attract more than a few of such wintering species as fox, song, and vesper sparrows, juncos, and brown creepers. On the other hand, it is far towards the northern limit of the winter range of tree swallows, gnatcatchers, blue-headed and white-eyed vireos, and orange-crowned warblers.

CHAPTER XIX

Amphibian with a Gun

A HUNTER IN WET, unstable surfaces of the coastlands may have occasion to be pessimistic about his surroundings, but not if he is in a scene of action. Let the snipe start rising on quaky ground ahead of him or the ducks begin flying past his blind, and the indeterminate, or fluidly constituted world all around him, is as exhilarating as the sights and sounds of woods, ridges, hills, or fields on a brisk autumn or winter day. Contagious vigor and volatility spread from the movements of the high-strung birds as they swing over the varied weave of waters, grasses, clean spongy places, and flattened, matted residue of marsh growths. In the flimsy yet inescapably commanding wastes, where each new mile confirms a first impression of intermingled land-almost-water and water-almost-land, of contours that wind and unwind among the blotched surfaces fading into the horizon or bound a smooth surface of the near-by patchwork, the sure presence and elemental intensity of the winged life permits of no indifference.

Practically considered, a hunter's relation to the marsh bird life is in reality a rather complicated one. As done in the very boggy marshes and intricate water surfaces towards the eastern part of the coast, duck-hunting, it should be observed, is not a casual sport but requires a good deal of outfitting and planning. For trappers and guides living nearest the duck haunts, to whom it is largely a matter of subsistence, it presents fewer practical problems. Otherwise, there are relatively few duck hunters, though in view of the concentration of population in southeastern Louisiana the number of consistent ones may appear at times to be large.

In the central and western parts of the coast of Louisiana, duckhunting is related more closely to the general life of communities. The distribution of the birds is not so contingent on peculiarities of topography as towards the east. Bayous and areas of low marsh are defined more clearly in the prairie-like, slightly elevated region which does not give way entirely to submerged areas near the coast and, therefore, are easier to reach.

A duckhunt in lower Louisiana begins usually a long way from its climactic point. The first step is to find a way to spots where ducks may be expected with reasonable assurance and where the hunter must have, as in most other duckhunting regions, a prior advantage by settling himself in a blind before the ducks arrive.

These are wily and fastidious birds. They do not come to a water surface without having first ascertained by those processes of intelligence, or consciousness, of which they are capable whether it offers choice food and at least relative safety. They have immense tracts of marshlands and shallows to select from, and, with their sure instinct, they make no mistake about finding the best. Outside of feeding hours, they may settle on any convenient and reasonably secure body of water, but then they are out of reach.

A spot where ducks are most in their element is not an ideal site for even a hunting camp. It is usually many acres and sometimes several miles from the main course of one of the bayous or other waterways that serve in so many parts of the lowlands as means of local travel and on or near which are the only human habitations ordinarily feasible in this region. The shallow basins in which ducks prefer to feed are connected rarely with one of these bayous of the marshlands except by the most devious water trails. Often they would be practically inaccessible if it were not that along certain parts of the route, hunters, guides, and camp owners have made what the French natives of Louisiana call "traverses" and "trainasses." These are mere ditches in which only the shallowest pirogue may be propelled by a pole to the pond or lagoon frequented by the ducks. At some points these ditches are too shallow to float the pirogue, and only vigorous pushing will keep it moving over the slimy, softly plastic ooze.

So reaching the blinds before daylight is an intrinsic and usually very intricate part of a lowland duckhunt, involving in some cases a transfer from a larger boat to the pirogue. It may, and often does, bring the monotony and hard work of paddling and poling or of sitting cramped and in shivering tenseness on cold mornings; extends an invitation for attack from mosquitoes if the atmosphere is at all mild; starts forebodings about the state of the weather; and, all in all, puts the hunter in a stoical rather than an expansive, or truly philosophical, frame of mind, one corner of which, usually the softest, he reserves for optimistic guesses about the likelihood of success. Despite the tedious approach to the blind, however, this prelude to dawn or sunrise is not all preoccupation or introspection. There are subdued sounds in water, air, and grass: the swish of a muskrat, suppressed notes of marsh birds, the whir of wings from snipe or duck disturbed in its night's lodgment, a distant quacking and splashing.

With the earliest light, shadowy forms appear just above the water and vegetation, vague and changeful, like great moths or beetles winging their way through the twilight. The time for reaching the blind is running out. Once there, the hunter has more chance to think pleasantly about his surroundings. He watches the horizon for the rim of the sun on a clear morning, begins to take account of flights of ducks starting to stretch across the heavens, and, if an observer of the law, settles down to await the time when he can try his hand on the birds that pass his blind, pull up at the sound of his call, or come over his decoys. A new tension, more agreeable than that of the long trip in the pirogue, begins to take hold of him.

If the morning is not rainy or very cold and there is a moderate wind to keep the ducks on a search for smooth water suited to their feeding, it can be considered perfect. Under such circumstances, it passes quickly enough for some and too soon for others. Next to an element of expectation, uncertain sequence of lulls and exciting action agitates the interest and the sense of encouragement for a hunter. Even a few chances for successful shots repay long waits and contribute to contentment with being in the wild, shifting picturesqueness of the marshes and a spectator of its strange life and incidents. Inquisitive rails and little marsh wrens come near the blind, coots and hell-divers swim unconcerned near-by, a snipe passes overhead now and then or plumps in a quickly spiraling turn and with a short note of finality into a watery bed of low grasses across the clumps of tall reeds and sedges. There may be little if any time for these chance sights. Teals, blackjacks, and other low-flying ducks drive in seemingly from nowhere past the blind or poise above the decoys with startling suddenness. There are flocks of ducks in the offing, moving with less than their usual directness and obviously on the lookout for a good pond or lagoon; the skillful use of the call may induce them to come in the hunter's direction. Even a flight that started as a blur against the clouds may reach the blind.

Whether success is little or considerable, true relaxation comes at midmorning. There is time to pick up the birds that have been left lying on the water out of convenient reach, to look over the bag, and to reflect on some of the occurrences and peculiarities of the morning's experience. If there is any occasion for restful satisfaction, this is the time for it. Likelihood of more shooting is over, preparation for leisurely return to the camp, with the advantage of daylight, is the next move. Rapidly now the pattern of ducks as they came within gunshot and the quickness and clearness of critical moments are becoming memories that blend slowly with mellowed outlooks across the marsh in the quiet and fullness of noon. Retrospect, not the speculation that filled the early hours, goes with the trip to camp, its promise of food and a time to lounge and absorb the easy tonic of the fading day.

In a long-famous duckhunting country like that of southern Louisiana, the art of making the crudest camp genuinely comfortable has gone a great way. Like the traits of many of the hunters, it reflects often a distinctive mixture of racial characteristics that at the same time can accomplish practical ends and preserve amenity and conviviality in an unusual degree. Expert duck shooters are numerous among the members of the clubs and the habitués of the camps, but many put more store by the hours of genial relaxation and a sociability that needs no prompting except commonly enjoyed experiences. Of the usual twenty-four hours that a duck hunter devotes to his recreation, from his arrival at camp one evening to departure the next, about two-thirds must be spent there. Making it a club, a home, an approach to the elements and a stronghold against them, all in one, is an accomplishment to which most duck hunters in the great realm of the marshes are fully equal.

CHAPTER XX

Summary Morning on the Marsh

A PART OF THE MARSH splotched with sloughs and little lakes is a sensitive expanse of green and tempered silver in the early freshness of summer mornings. The perfect type of these surfaces lies between tide wastes and the last cypress brakes of the coast belt and shares somewhat the qualities of each. In warmer parts of the year it is the rarely invaded home of such inhabitants as muskrats, marsh hens, gallinules, herons, and red-winged blackbirds.

Neglected logging or drainage canals in the rear of plantations on the older reclaimed lands are approaches well matched with these rich and colorful wastes. The course of a waterway of this kind begins in the corridor of cypress and other swamp trees and runs for several miles in this envelopment of shadow before joining some bayou of the open marsh. If started in time to reach a destination by early morning, a trip along the canal may be nearly all in darkness. Toward its end, the curtained view distinctive of the route begins to take shape. Spectral outlines of bordering trees and gray moss grow faintly definable in the approach of dawn. A pale light spreads over the treetops and outlines them against the faded colors of the sky. The shadowy water begins to assume multiple tones. The world is in suspense, there are mere quivers of light and motion in the air. The first perceptible breeze, the earliest birds seen as they fly high or low across the canal ahead of the boat are starting signals of the whole wonderful spectacle of sunrise and the awakening of life.

The stir on the marsh in the early hours is not easily forgotten. The colors alone repay the effort of reaching it. There is a field of placid, green herbage and pearly water, with soft tints of rose and ashy blue. In the full light of morning it unfolds a filigree of the flowers of wild mallow—pink, saffron, light carmine, varied with the blue and white of other marsh blossoms.

In the quiet and the tempered brightness of morning, the scene is fluid, smooth, and iridescent. There is no flaw, nothing unbalanced yet by the widening day. A wrinkling on the water and the slight swaying of the reeds prelude the return of life throughout the marsh. A dazzlingly brilliant gallimule, the embodiment of chromatic splendor, or a more sedately colored rail steps from within the thatch of flags and bulrushes to the water's edge. The strange, concerted voices of their hidden companions give momentum to the trend of the morning. The clatter of the rail, the resonant and oddly musical calls of the gallinules, like the striking of a single note on a stringed instrument, echo sonorously amid the floating and the upright vegetation of the watery plain. The livelier notes of red-winged blackbirds and the gibbering, gurgling calls of the boat-tailed grackles sharpen the realization of an encircling life with which the marsh is filled. Its most musical expression is the song of the marsh wren, trilling with a liquid cadence in clusters of reeds and rushes.

As the morning heightens, small terns from the islands and outer marshes of the coast ride lightly on the incoming sea breezes, whistling, chattering, dipping deftly to the shallow water. They have brought the spell of the open shore to the more placid reaches of sheltered waters. When they arrive, the morning is at its height. More and more the red-winged blackbirds utter their musical calls and rapidly chattered notes. Herons, bound from one feeding ground to another, are everywhere against the sky. The other marsh birds answer each other across the luxuriant, oozy levels. There is no discord apparent in this exuberant life but merely rising elation and animation before the somnolence of noon descends upon it. It starts again in a minor pitch in the later hours of the afternoon and subsides within the cover of dusk to await the coming of another dawn.

CHAPTER XXI

In the Bends of the Mississippi

THE LAST TWO OR THREE hundred miles in the course of the Mississippi are a maze of peculiarities and incongruities. In all the lowlands of Louisiana on which it borders or through which it flows, the river is really the creator rather than a mere aspect of the landscape. Man-made levees and other means of flood control have put an end to its spreading periodically over a great region and depositing heavy loads of silt, substance of new or more uniform areas of land. While the scenery is now established beyond all likelihood of change, excepting, of course, the tip of the delta, it is always interesting to remember how it originated.

Unlike the surfaces now reclaimed from overflow and new land-building, the fringe of land between the levee and the margin of the river at ordinary stages is a surface over which nature's control is absolute and perpetual. High water covers the fine, gray sand of this ledge but seldom long enough to destroy its character as the site of a strange, adventitious forest sometimes of surprisingly great proportions and of exceptional beauty and richness. Except on the lowest margins, where the growth is largely of willows, it has a clean floor, well spaced, finely formed trees, most of them small. Cottonwood and sycamore are usually the largest kinds, while hackberry and honey locust, or thorn tree, are the prevailing ones, although several others, such as southern red and water oaks, are occasional. Although water may stand in low spots, this is a light-soiled and well-drained woodland when the river is low and offers little if any attraction for the cypress and swamp tupelo. The live oak, which flourishes only on land high enough to escape ordinary overflow, has no place here. These areas, known as "battures," are thus uniform stretches of purely deciduous woodland, the trees spare and trim in winter, luxuriant but not tangled in the warmer months. The surface is easily traversed at most times if the river does not rise over it.

The casual woods along the shores of the river are characteristic to within less than a hundred miles of its mouth or, in fact, until the natural banks sink to within a foot or so of sea level. These peculiar collections of trees add immeasurably to the picturesqueness of the flowing bends and lakelike expanses that sweep from point to point of the stream, though they are to be seen, of course, only outside or from the top of the levee.

The levee on either side of the river hides a view of

the stream from the rich, level farm and plantation lands behind it. The same circumstance renders the stream and its immediate borders when seen from the edge of the batture a composition complete in itself. In the hot, still days of late summer, the wide-bending reaches of glassy water, with strong reflections of blue and opal from a clear sky, blend in soft, mirage-like borders with a mellowed, varied green of compact foliage that shelves back and up to the levee. In spring or early summer, the river may have menaced the whole countryside, even that behind high levees, but now in this season of placid smoothness and peaceful drifting and glowingly verdant margins it is a serene and colorful expanse, as impeturbable as a mill pond. Across its surface, brightly mirroring the clouds, and among the willows and low, forest-like growths moves the quiet breath of the bright lowlands.

The copse-like growths beside the terraces of gray and creamy sand at the river's edge are obscure and little visited and, though within hail of homes, roads, stores, or fields, are still an elemental world—trees, water, sand—in view only of those who walk on the levee, go on rare occasion to the water's edge, or move along or across the river in a boat. The full significance of its beauty and completeness when the river stage is low and verdure covers the shores does not become apparent until one is in its midst. Then new lines and contrasts in its surface swing into the perspective and an unmarred picture takes shape from the simplest of components. The bareness of winter, however, or the brimming, ruffled, colorless current of the river in spring deprives the view between the shores of the singular attractiveness that comes to it on clear summer or fall days.

The fertile Louisiana countryside west of the river and partly that on the east is one of haphazard scenes but, whether neglected or cultivated, is at least uniform in being almost perfectly level. Fields of sugar cane and rice towards the south and of cotton towards the north, interspersed with corn and various secondary crops, stretch away from the levee for various distances to a background of moist or swampy woods, where the elevations are slightly less than in the immediate neighborhood of the stream. This strange reversal of ordinary riverland topography has its explanation, as does everything else in this peculiar country, in the fact that in a former epoch the river spread unrestrained during its high stages and left the deepest deposits nearest its main course. Rainfall in the area drains back from the river, sometimes finding its way into former outlets, now almost currentless streams, cut off from the river and filled up or become shallow for parts of their extent with local sediments and humus. Such are Bayous Plaquemine, Lafourche, and several others. The former course of one of these, Bayou Manchac, is hardly distinguishable today.

Never have streams entered the Mississippi in the southern Louisiana lowlands, as the watershed has been always away from it instead of towards it. At the northern edge of the lowlands, Red River discharges partly into the Mississippi through an involvement of channels that open also into the Atchafalaya, a former outlet or possibly at one time the main course of the Mississippi from this point to the Gulf of Mexico, a waterway that has kept its bed scoured deep in the alluvium and that has at some points a sounding of two hundred feet, making it probably one of the deepest streams in the world.

The former outlets of the Mississippi below the confluence of Red River are more nearly like long sloughs than active streams today. Their inertness makes them very typical of the rich, flat region over which they extend. As seen across cleared or lightly wooded lands in summer, they trace against the brilliant verdure of these lowlands a ribbon of vegetation of still more intense hues.

An irregularly level terrain buried in luxuriant growths is distinctive of the district of crescent-shaped lakes near the Mississippi in central and northern Louisiana. These bodies of water are remnants of former channels of the river that became separated from its main flow when its course changed and have survived as curved, lakelike segments of the stream, the ends separated from the new course of the river by the processes of sedimentation. The surrounding lands reveal the history of the river's influence, show where it has scoured or where it has brought new deposits, leaving a picturesqueness of contour that emphasizes the varying tones of rich vegetation. Such scenes, like a mosaic of thickets, fallow lands, luxuriant crops, and low, green banks, have a rich, pastoral beauty. The most striking example of this type of country is the False River section in Pointe Coupée parish, where the small, bright homes of a farming population mostly French in extraction add a sharper delineation to the landscape and recall scenes of European countryside.

CHAPTER XXII

October Beauty of the Duck Grounds

TRAVEL IN A SMALL BOAT along the bayous and canals that trace a strange course through the open boglands of Louisiana is especially wonderful on bright, still October days. The season is that halcyon time when a wide, colorful peacefulness envelops the spaces that become in winter the gathering grounds of waterfowl. The hunting season has not started and the mild beauty of the wet, meadowy flats is undisturbed. Some of their intricacy dissolves, and in the clearness of the sunshine outlines radiate in an untangled veining of water lanes and broad, fluid beds of marsh plants, level and elastic. In these final days of bland weather, the intrinsic character of the liquid surfaces and colors takes on its most extended fluency, a flexible weaving of vegetation and water, green fusing with pale gold, silver with pearly azure.

Things that make the marshes unforgettable in the warm radiance of October are not merely their bright waters and mellowed growths but the touches of peculiar richness and fullness that flow from the strength and maturity of nature's trend at this season. The enchantment grows mile after mile, the incandescence of light on the shining surfaces of the water, the molten haze at the far, vague shore of a marsh lake, thinly margined with small cypresses or live oaks. There is an eager life abroad in the outspread, ripened world. Coots are there, newly arrived in the wake of cool nights, swimming quietly in the sheltered pools and inner bayous. Teal and snipe that have led the winter incursion of marsh-loving birds break from their covers. Late-lingering shore birds are traced by their quietly reverberating notes. Close at hand is the sound of fluttering and splashing in a reed-bound lagoon. Scene by scene, happening by happening, the many enticements of the marsh on a golden day outgrow even those of mountain and forest. It is a realm over which the eye can travel far, yet find some always new hint of novelty or mystery.

Turning points or other places notable along a familiar route through the heart of the marshy lands have a fresh significance in the autumn day. The keeper of the "lily boom" at the mouth of a sluggish, shallow bayou, filled with a raft of the disastrously naturalized water-hyacinths, to be kept back as far as possible from the more traveled waterways, has the feeling of the day. He is communicative about the coming and going of the earliest ducks, the state of a near-by feeding ground for snipe, an invasion of coots, or *"poules d'eau"* in a hidden lagoon and their obliteration of the food plants that might have served later for the attraction of ducks. A widened shallow where herons gather in fine weather glistens brilliantly, but in place of the more numerous company that go here in the warmest months there are only a few birds. They are making their last stand among the still green pickerelweeds, marsh grasses, and low rushes, advancing on the frogs and small fish that have not taken yet to the deeper waters or mire.

Sparsely scattered bayou-side thickets of low willows, familiar resorts of red-winged blackbird and boat-tailed grackles, now offer a stopping place to a chance vireo or warbler, strayed from its migratory course and conspicuous but restive in the thinning and yellowing leaves, caught in a perplexity, yet not faring too badly in the mildness and quiet of its temporary surroundings.

If a large lake is part of the route, a trip through the marshy spaces on a clear October day is remembered as a great encirclement of shining blue and translucent gold, an inundation of transparent brightness, from center to margin, that rests equally on the water and the purpled, fugitive rim of low growth at the horizon. The bayou that continues the watery trail beyond the lake may pass a curving ridge of picturesquely massed live oaks, lending stability and intimacy to the vague ness of the open reaches. Intersections and mazes of other waterways bring in a new suggestion of remoteness and wilder reaches irresistible to waterbirds. It is the brightness of the sun-bathed lake and its hazy shores, however, that has created an unfading memory. It is the final touch in the more durable wonders of autumn.

CHAPTER XXIII

Rare or Striking Birds

No BOOK DESCRIPTION can visualize beforehand a first meeting in the field with a particular species of bird. There is no telling in just what kind of places and under what circumstances it will become a reality, a living presence. An acquaintance with very familiar species comes without search and is a kind of common inheritance of observing persons, but discovery of birds that live secluded or unusual lives is very different. There is no way of anticipating where or how they will appear.

I recall seeing for the first time those less conspicuous thrushes, the gray-cheeked and the olive-backed. On many days, especially in spring, several companions and I had explored a locality just outside of New Orleans that was formerly a perfect resort for the typical avifauna of the region. After a few seasons, we believed that we had seen every species that could be expected to appear there regularly. We had tramped and scrambled, waded and beaten about in the thickets, sloughs, canebrakes, old fields, pasture lands, willow ponds, plantation edges, and rich level woodland in an area of some twenty square miles on so many Saturdays during the migrations that there was no distinctive acre that we had not crossed under many conditions. Then, one year, on April 20, when migration was going into its final period and almost its end for a majority of species familiarly present, the two friends with me that day, having left me to go through a stretch of typical thick, moist woodland, reappeared with a message of discovery in their eyes. To confirm it, they had with them a new specimen, one of the slender, tawny-olive and creamy white gray-cheeked thrushes. There was nothing in the books to show that it should not be in this locality in spring. It could hardly fail to pass here in its migrations; so why shouldn't we find it? But in such matters, as in others, seeing is believing. No book that we knew about had explained that its migration is a late one and that its appearance in rather large numbers at this time would not be really remarkable; nor did we have the benefit of the actual experience of other students in neighboring regions, as this was before the days of widely published records of bird distribution and migration. Being all unprepared for the experience, we felt the elation of receiving an unexpected gift.

After learning personally, rather than vicariously, of the existence of this species, we progressed rapidly to the knowledge that with its close relative, the olive-backed thrush, it makes up a rather numerous company among the migrants of late spring and is commonest for a short while in copses and bushy places rather than in the higher growths of the woodlands. Many collect even in stands of tall weeds.

When I had become conversant with the presence and movements of these birds by day, I discovered that great numbers of them pass at low altitudes over the coast section on warm, wet nights culminating a particularly mild spell that has induced heavy northward migration. Among the many bird voices coming from above, a surprisingly large number are the low, whistling calls of the thrushes. They seem to be at an elevation of less than two or three hundred feet. On clear nights preceding the rain they fly at much greater heights and are not heard readily, if at all. Mixed with their calls are those of green and night herons, shorebirds, nighthawks, indigo buntings, catbirds, Wilson thrushes, which have a clearer, less guttural note than the other thrushes, and many warblers not identifiable under the circumstances.

Usually on the day following one of these heavy flights of migrants, especially if the weather has cleared with falling temperature and rising barometer, one may see a good many of the thrushes heard the night before. They may be found secluded in thickets of young willows and other low growths, uttering occasionally their peculiar notes. The difference between the two species is not easy to make out in the field except under favorable circumstances. The gray-cheeked thrush is more nearly pure white below, especially about the throat and cheeks. It is more definitely brown or tawny than olive on the back.

In the woods where my friends found the gray-cheeked thrush there was another bird, Swainson's warbler, that we overlooked for some time. Its short, penetrating song, with a peculiarly wild inflection yet resembling the notes of one or two other species and mingling with all the bird music of these woods, did not register in our consciousness at first as a distinct song, part of which was somewhat like that of the hooded warbler. Once we had realized, however, that there was a different singer among the better known ones, we strained our eyes and ears for positive knowledge of the performer. The center of our search was a thicket of wild cane in a close growth of red and water oaks, sweet gums, elms, and other trees of less swampy parts of these Mississippi River lowlands, which in this case had been formed by deposits of a crevasse. My companion on this occasion forced his way through the tangled cane at a point where he had heard one of the birds singing and finally secured the first specimen of Swainson's warbler that we had ever seen.

After we had made sure of where to look for the newly discovered bird, which was usually at a height of a few feet in the cane or the smallest saplings and the lower limbs of larger trees, we became familiar with it and failed rarely to observe it during April. On one occasion, during the middle of the month, I saw probably twenty in one day, most of them in the wetter part of the woods. While a few individuals may have nested where we found the species, it was there chiefly in migration. Swainson's warbler is one of the most inconspicuously and soberly marked of its family in North America. The upper parts are wood brown, with an olive cast, the underparts and a streak over the eye dull whitish.

Rarity, as applied to the presence of any species of bird, is a relative matter. Some kinds are rare everywhere, even in their chosen haunts. Others may be so except in a very limited area or at a specified season. A wild turkey in the Louisiana marshes at any time would be a decided rarity and a blue goose there in July would be equally such. A bird far out of its usual range or its usual type of habitat is not really a rarity but an accident, as the occurrence in Louisiana of the scarlet ibis, the Inca dove, and the golden-crowned sparrow, all of which have been recorded there. The interesting rare birds are those that may be expected in a particular region with some degree of probability, those that are inherently rare, or those that have a very uncertain range. Some such birds in Louisiana are cinnamon teal, whistling swans, Harris hawks, whooping

[182]

and sandhill cranes, roseate spoonbills, reddish egrets, black rails, snowy plovers, stilt and buff-breasted sand-pipers, ground doves, olive-sided flycatchers, and Bachman's, Cape May, and mourning warblers. There are fully a score of others equally or more unlikely to be seen. Those named are some of the very interesting ones, either because of their beauty, unusual appearance, or great uncertainty as to when and where they will appear. Most bird-lovers would find unusual satisfaction in coming across any of them.

The now almost extinct ivory-billed woodpecker, which was always more characteristic of deep forests in the higher river basins than in the coastal area, is a rare sight not because of uncertainty as to where it may be found but, on the contrary, because the character of its habitat is too fixed. The larvae of beetles peculiar to very old and extensive growths of ash, elm, sweet gum, hickory, and water and overcup oaks are a requisite in the diet of this species, and a decreasing extent of such woodland remains in Louisiana. Even though its food supply should continue to exist in more limited expanses of this kind of forest, the ivory-billed woodpecker is too shy a bird to prosper in a very restricted haunt.

One may go for years without seeing some of the rarer birds and then come across them in a most surprising way. The only time that I ever saw an olive-sided flycatcher in Louisiana was when I sat one mid-

August afternoon on an upstairs porch overlooking river woodlands in a piney locality, with nothing further from my mind than seeing some unusual bird on this drowsy day in late summer. Yet a casual glance towards a pine about a hundred feet away brought within view a bird of somewhat striking appearance perched on a conspicuous dead branch. A closer look showed it to resemble a wood pewee but to be considerably larger, with a tuft of light feathers sticking from under its wing on the side towards me, almost as if for the convenience of an observer, for this is a characteristic point in recognition of the olive-sided flycatcher. While breeding far north, this species migrates very early in the fall. Correspondingly, its northward migration is late in spring. The few that have been observed near the Gulf Coast have been present at these seasons.

As a result of very cold weather, certain birds typical of bare winter woods and countryside dip southward sometimes into the coastlands. It is strange to find them in what might have been a few days earlier an almost summery environment, where easy-living birds of a temperate climate disperse freely and familiarly among live oaks, sheltered swamps, and heavy, half-green undergrowth. These newcomers have a hardy briskness and restlessness that are lacking somewhat in the colder weather in the case of their new-found companions.

The purple finch is one of the rather rare and irregular winter visitors. The deep rosy or nearly crimson plumage of the male is entirely different from that of any other bird ever appearing in the coast belt. It is not flaming, like the dress of the tanager and the cardinal, but has a glowing warmth that complements the soberer colors of winter. The dingy female, resembling the same sex in the common house sparrow, might escape notice very easily. As a rule, purple finches reaching these far southern surroundings are in small, widely scattered flocks. They are seldom so numerous that their presence is not always something of a surprise, yet some of them may linger even into the early spring without apparent urge to return to the more northern localities from which snow and cold blasts had driven them. They are easiest to observe when they are feeding on the leaf-buds of oak, elm, beech, sweet gum, and other trees among the pines or in swampy woods. Unless absorbed in their repasts, they move from one spot to another with the abrupt, rapid flight of the house sparrow.

A small finch, the pine siskin, or linnet, enters the lowlands and other country near the coast during or following the colder weather. It wanders more widely than the purple finch, may remain somewhat later, and appears in larger, more compact flocks, which keep well up in bare trees or those on which the buds open early. They are almost constantly in motion and have a continuous, musical twittering something like that of the goldfinch. The siskin has a flaxen and dusky plumage, which resembles in color tone, but not in pattern, that of the goldfinch, as if it had acquired the winter suit of that species worn shabby and streaky. In its nesting districts, the siskin prefers evergreen forests, but it is decidedly a bird of deciduous trees on its visits to the coast.

On very rare occasions other finches with far northern breeding ranges have been known to come as far south as the purple finch and the siskin. One is the red crossbill, which has appeared at least once near the northern shore of Lake Pontchartrain. The snow bunting, a breeder in the arctic region, has come also to the same general locality. The record of its occurrence there rests on a museum specimen. This species is not to be confused, of course, with the common snowbird, or slate-colored junco, which is fairly common in winter in the higher woods of the coast section.

The hint of half-wild lands and the more remote countryside goes with the presence of the blue grosbeak. This large relative of the indigo bunting slips into and out of open situations at irregular times in spring and fall. It is likely to be about in the latter part of April as it passes inland to its breeding haunts in such places as the pine hills of the interior. In late August and in September, it is on its way back, sometimes visiting the edges of rice fields and feeding on the ripened grain. It has a sharp call-note louder than that of the indigo bunting but does not sing in the lowlands. It reserves for its nesting places a short song of rather rare quality resembling the notes of both the tanager and the indigo bunting. The male is a pure, deep blue, with a small patch of chestnut on the wing. The female is pale brown, another point of resemblance between this species and the indigo bunting.

Although growing constantly rarer, the swallow-tailed kite is still a characteristic figure in the less accessible wooded swamplands of southern Louisiana, particularly about lakes or in heavily wooded bottoms near bayous and small rivers. The slender gracefulness of this large black and white bird is a fitting complement of the strange, immobile picturesqueness of cypress-bordered lakes and heavy belts of swamp woodland. As a member of the falcon family that feeds only on snakes, frogs, small rodents, and large insects, it should be entirely free from the prejudice directed usually against raptorial birds. Its beauty and comparative rarity, also, should make it safe from firearms. It has an equally harmless relative, the Mississippi kite, that is considerably commoner, though not resorting to as remote places. Some years ago, I saw an unusual number of these kites soaring one late summer day over cornfields and waste lands between the other fields of a Mississippi River sugar plantation and the nearest woods. The handsome, slate-gray birds, with several of the swallow-tailed kites among them, were a spectacle not likely to be repeated. The great numbers of grasshoppers and cicadas, or "locusts," were the attraction causing the assemblage.

A few birds of almost exclusively tropical distribution go as far north as the Gulf Coast. The common ani and the groove-billed ani, which are allied to the cuckoos, are two of the most interesting of these. Strangely enough, they are almost as likely to occur in winter as in summer. They are the size of grackles and are a somewhat less glossy, much less iridescent black, and have stout, high-profiled, horizontally compressed bills, rather like a parrot's. A simple-minded native, trying to describe an ani to a bird student in his locality, called it a "little black polly."

Anis are decidedly uncommon in southern Louisiana, and their appearance seems to be limited to the fields and groves nearest the coast. Most reports of them have come from the last cultivable lands in Plaquemines parish on the west side of the Mississippi River.

Finding new birds in a familiar region, however common the same kinds may be elsewhere, is always a true delight. Search for them in lower Louisiana has an added incentive because there is always the possibility of coming across stragglers or unusual migrants from tropical or from far northern haunts—even strangers from the West. And even though rare discoveries come only at long intervals, they persist in the memory, postponing indefinitely the day when surprises seem beyond all reasonable hope.

8593